SpringerBriefs in Information Systems

Series Editor
Jörg Becker, Münster, Germany

More information about this series at http://www.springer.com/series/10189

Diogo R. Ferreira

A Primer on Process Mining

Practical Skills with Python and Graphviz

Second Edition

 Springer

Diogo R. Ferreira
Instituto Superior Técnico
University of Lisbon
Oeiras, Portugal

ISSN 2192-4929 ISSN 2192-4937 (electronic)
SpringerBriefs in Information Systems
ISBN 978-3-030-41818-2 ISBN 978-3-030-41819-9 (eBook)
https://doi.org/10.1007/978-3-030-41819-9

This Springer imprint is published by the registered company Springer Nature Switzerland AG.
The registered company address is: Gewerbestrasse 11, 6330 Cham, Switzerland

Preface to the Second Edition

As we enter January 2020, Python 2 has reached its end of life; so an update to Python 3 becomes useful. I also took this opportunity to correct a few (surprisingly very few) issues in the text. I would like to thank my student Iezalde Lopes and my colleague José Borbinha for having spotted these small details.

Lisbon, Portugal
January 2020

Diogo R. Ferreira

Preface to the First Edition

Over the years, I had to introduce a number of M.Sc. and Ph.D. students to the topic of process mining. Invariably, it was difficult to find a concise introduction to the topic, despite the fact that some of the fundamental ideas of process mining are quite simple. In principle, it should not be necessary to go through a series of research papers in order to get a good grasp of those ideas.

On the other hand, I did not want my students to start using ProM[1] or Disco[2] right away, without understanding what is happening behind the scenes. Instead, I would prefer to provide them with the working knowledge that would allow them to implement some simple process mining techniques on their own, even if only in a rudimentary form. It always seemed to me that being able to implement something is the best way to develop a solid understanding of a new topic.

The main goal of this book is to explain the core ideas of process mining and to show how these ideas can be implemented using just some basic tools that are available to any computer scientist or data scientist. One of such tools is the Python programming language, which has become very popular since it allows writing complex programs in a clear and concise form. Another tool that is very useful is the Graphviz library, which is able to display graphs and automatically calculate their layout without requiring the programmer to do so. Graphviz provides an effortless way to visualize the results of many process mining techniques.

Before going further, some disclaimers are in order; namely, this book is not meant to be a reference on process mining. In that sense, it would be very incomplete, since we will be using only a simplified version of a very small subset of process mining techniques. Also, the text does not delve into a wide variety of process models that can be generated by those techniques. Here, we will be using

---

[1]http://www.promtools.org/.

[2]https://fluxicon.com/disco/.

graphs (both directed and undirected, but just plain graphs) without getting into more sophisticated process modeling languages, such as Petri nets[3] and BPMN.[4]

Nevertheless, this bare-bones approach should suffice to provide a feeling for what process mining is, while developing some skills that will definitely be useful in practice.

I prepared this text to be a very first introduction to process mining, and hence I called it a *primer*. After this, the reader can jump more confidently to the existing literature, namely the book by Wil van der Aalst,[5] and the extensive set of research publications in this field. I hope that this text will contribute towards a deeper understanding of process mining tools and techniques.

Lisbon, Portugal   Diogo R. Ferreira
February 2017

---

[3]http://www.informatik.uni-hamburg.de/TGI/PetriNets/.

[4]http://www.bpmn.org/.

[5]See [18] in the list of references on page 95.

Contents

Chapter 1
Event Logs

Organizations have information systems that record activities of interest, such as the registration of a new customer, the sale of a product, the approval of a purchase request, the processing of a payment, etc. All of these activities result in one or more events being recorded in some information system.

In the past, such events were mainly used for the purpose of record-keeping, accounting, auditing, etc. More recently, organizations have started leveraging those data for business analytics, namely the kind of analysis that can be performed with data warehouses and online analytical processing (OLAP).[1]

Process mining is concerned with a different goal: the aim of process mining is to take advantage of event data in order to understand how an organization works. For example, with process mining it is possible to discover the sequence of tasks that are performed in a certain business process, and also the interactions that take place between the participants in that process.

Analyzing business processes in this way is important for a number of reasons, namely to assess the internal performance of an organization, to raise awareness of how people work and how they interact with each other, and ultimately to identify opportunities for efficiency improvements and better usage of resources.

The starting point for process mining is an *event log*. This event log may be the actual log of some information system (e.g. the log file of an application server), or it may be a log file that is built from historical data recorded in a database, for example. Whatever the source, the data in an event log must have (or must be converted to) a specific structure. The goal of this chapter is to explain that structure. However, to understand why an event log has such structure, it is useful to introduce some general concepts about business processes first.

---

[1]For a reference on this topic, see e.g. [16].

© The Author(s) 2020
D. R. Ferreira, *A Primer on Process Mining*, SpringerBriefs in Information Systems,
https://doi.org/10.1007/978-3-030-41819-9_1

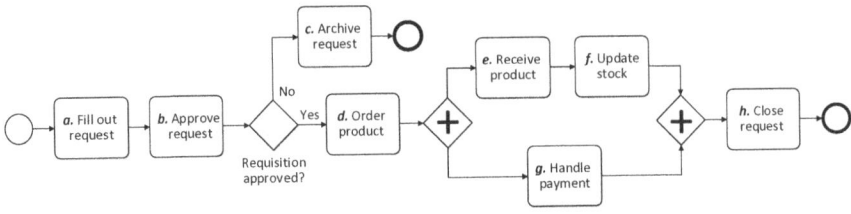

Fig. 1 Example of a process model (adapted from [3]). Adapted from Computers in Industry, 70, Ferreira, D.R., Vasilyev, E.: Using logical decision trees to discover the cause of process delays from event logs, pp 194-207, © 2015, with permission from Elsevier

1.1 Process Model vs. Process Instances

It is often said that a business process is a set of activities which, collectively, produce some output that is of value for a business organization or for its customers.[2] Our main interest here is to understand how the process unfolds over time while being executed. In particular, it is common to think of a business process as sequence of discrete steps, called *activities*.

An activity is a unit of work that makes sense from a business point of view. For example, creating a purchase order or approving a purchase request are examples of what could be seen as activities in a purchase process. Figure 1 shows an example of how such process could look like.

Here, an employee fills out a request form (activity a) and sends it to a manager for approval (activity b). If the request is not approved, it is archived (activity c) and the process ends. If the request is approved, the product is ordered from a supplier (activity d). Then two things happen at the same time: the warehouse receives the product (activity e) and updates the stock (activity f), while the accounting department takes care of payment to the supplier (activity g). When these activities are over, the request is closed (activity h), and the process ends.

Figure 1 shows a representation of the process that is usually called a *process model*. It is a graphical, step-by-step description of the process in a form that is similar to a flowchart. In this particular example, it is a model of what happens when an employee wants to buy something.

The process model describes the sequence of activities in a general, abstract form. Every time someone wants to buy something in this organization, there will be an *instance* of this process for that particular purchase request.

The instances of this process may have different behaviors. For example, suppose that there two purchase requests, where one is approved and the other is not. Then these two instances will follow different paths in the model of Fig. 1: the first will go through activity d and the second will end up in activity c.

---

[2]For similar definitions, see [27] and [1].

Even if two instances follow the same path, there may be differences in their behavior. For example, since activity g is in parallel with e and f, it may happen that g is performed before e and f in one instance, and in another instance it is performed after e and f, or even in between them.

With process mining, it is possible to analyze how this process is performed in the organization. This is useful for a number of different purposes, such as determining the percentage of purchase requests that get approved, discovering the most frequent sequences of activities, estimating the time that it takes for the process to complete, etc. In addition, sometimes it happens that a process instance displays a behavior that does not comply with the model, such as executing activities in a different order, or even executing activities that are not in the original model.

It is in these scenarios that process mining becomes a valuable tool to discover how the process is *actually* being executed, as opposed to how the process was *supposed* to be executed. In some scenarios, it will be possible to compare the behavior of a process model defined at design-time with the behavior of process instances observed at run-time, and this is also a important topic of research in the field of process mining.[3] Here, we will be focusing mostly on the problem of discovering the run-time behavior of business processes.

1.2 Task Allocation

Following the example of the purchase process above, one could imagine an organization with many employees, with several people trying to buy things every now and then, or even at the same time. The business process will be instantiated multiple times, one for each purchase request, and several of those process instances may be active simultaneously at any given point in time.

Suppose that in one process instance the product is being ordered, while in another process instance the product has already been received, and in yet another process instance the request is still waiting for approval, etc. All of these process instances are active at the same time, as people are working on them.

Additionally, suppose that there are eight people (employees) involved in this process. We will refer to them generically as *users*. If there are four process instances to be executed, then the allocation of all of these activities to the eight users could be as shown in Fig. 2.

In these four process instances, two of them get approved and the other two do not. We leave it as an exercise for the reader to determine how many instances of each activity $a, b, \ldots, h$ are there to be performed.

Each instance of these activities will have to be performed by someone. We refer to each of these activity instances as a *task*. Figure 2 shows how these tasks have been distributed among users.

---

[3]This topic is usually referred to as *conformance checking* [12].

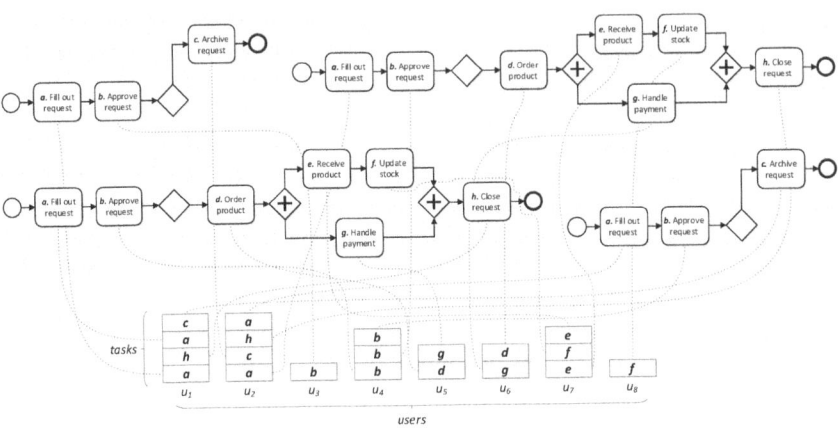

Fig. 2 Allocation of tasks to users

It appears that this distribution is somewhat unbalanced, and this may be due to several reasons, such as the length or complexity of each task, the responsibilities of each user, the fact that some users may not be available at a certain moment, etc. There may be some level of unpredictability in the allocation of work.

Also, Fig. 2 shows the allocation of tasks to users as if all tasks had been pre-assigned at once. In reality, such allocation is dynamic and it happens on-the-fly as the process is being executed. Usually, tasks are assigned to users at the moment when those tasks need to be performed. Typically, this occurs when the previous task has been completed.

For example, if a purchase request is approved (as a result of activity b), then the next activity is d and it will be necessary to assign a new task d to some user. On the other hand, if the request is not approved, then the next activity to be assigned is c and the choice of user may be different.

Task allocation is another aspect of business processes that can be analyzed through process mining techniques. Namely, it is possible to discover the workload assigned to each user, and also how users interact and collaborate with each other when performing a business process, i.e. who passes work to whom and who works together with whom on each process instance.

1.3 Identifying the Process Instances

In practice, every process instance has some kind of unique identifier. For example, in a sales process, each order has a unique number; in a technical support process, each reported problem has a ticket number; and so on.

Similarly, in the purchase process above, each purchase request will have a unique number. The purpose of having a unique identifier is to be able to track the status and progress of each process instance.

In the purchase process above, an employee will want to know whether a certain purchase request has been approved or not. For that purpose, the unique identifier of the purchase request must be provided in order to distinguish it from other purchase requests. This applies to other kinds of business process as well. For example, in a technical support process, it is usually required to provide an issue number in any follow-up contacts regarding a previously reported problem.

In the context of process mining, the identifier of a process instance is usually called the *case id*. The reason for this is that, in many business scenarios, each process instance is referred to as a *case*, so the term *case id* became popular.

This may be easier to understand if we think in terms of a patient that goes to a hospital, for example. There will be several tasks performed by different people (nurses, doctors, etc.) while taking care of a patient. The patient is referred to as a *case*, and of course there will be many different cases to take care of, as new patients keep entering the hospital. In this context, treating a patient (i.e. handling a certain *case*) is equivalent to executing an instance of some clinical process.

In the purchase process above, we can also look at each purchase request as a different *case* that needs to be handled, and we can identify each process instance by its *case id*, which is the purchase request number.

1.4   Recording Events in an Event Log

When a user performs a task in a process instance, this represents an event of interest that should be recorded. Gathering such events will allow a subsequent analysis with process mining techniques. When a significant number of such events have been recorded, we refer to that collection of events as an *event log*.

For the purpose of process mining, each event that is recorded in an event log should contain at least the following information:

- a *case id*, which identifies the process instance;
- a *task* name, which identifies the activity that has been performed;
- a *user* name, which identifies the participant who performed the task;
- a *timestamp*, which indicates the date and time when the task was completed.

Table 1 shows a sample event log that resulted from the execution of three instances of the purchase process. The event log contains the four columns mentioned above, and the events are presented in chronological order (increasing timestamp), which reflects the order in which they were recorded.

The events from these three process instances are somewhat intertwined. Namely, events from case id 1 are interspersed with events from case id 2, and the same happens with the events from case ids 2 and 3. This often happens in practice, when there are multiple process instances running concurrently.

Table 1 Example of an event log

Case id	Task	User	Timestamp
1	a	u_1	2016-04-09 17:36:47
1	b	u_3	2016-04-11 09:11:13
1	d	u_6	2016-04-12 10:00:12
1	e	u_7	2016-04-12 18:21:32
1	f	u_8	2016-04-13 13:27:41
2	a	u_2	2016-04-14 08:56:09
2	b	u_3	2016-04-14 09:36:02
2	d	u_5	2016-04-15 10:16:40
1	g	u_6	2016-04-18 19:14:14
2	g	u_6	2016-04-19 15:39:15
1	h	u_2	2016-04-19 16:48:16
2	e	u_7	2016-04-20 14:39:45
2	f	u_8	2016-04-22 09:16:16
3	a	u_2	2016-04-25 08:39:24
2	h	u_1	2016-04-26 12:19:46
3	b	u_4	2016-04-29 10:56:14
3	c	u_1	2016-04-30 15:41:22

In this sample event log, the tasks and users have been abbreviated with a single letter and number. This was done mostly for simplicity, but it should be noted that task names and user names in an event log are somewhat arbitrary. In some scenarios, they can be anonymized due to privacy reasons.

Regardless of the actual names, what matters is their relationships, such as the order in which they appear in the event log, and whether they appear within the same case id or not. It is these relationships that process mining techniques will focus on, in order to discover the behavior of the business process.

1.5 Event Logs in CSV Format

In practice, an event log may take different forms. The simplest form is a text file, but an event log may also be stored in the form of a database table, for example. In any case, it should be possible to export an event log as a text file.

The most common format for storing and exporting event logs is the well-known text format known as CSV (comma-separated values). This format is commonly used in spreadsheet applications, for example.

In a CSV file, each event is usually stored in a single line, and the four fields (*case id*, *task*, *user*, and *timestamp*) are separated by some punctuation symbol, usually a comma (,). If the comma is used as a decimal symbol or as a digit grouping symbol, then it is common to separate the fields by a semicolon (;) instead.

Listing 1 Event log in CSV format

```
 1    1;a;u1;2016-04-09 17:36:47
 2    1;b;u3;2016-04-11 09:11:13
 3    1;d;u6;2016-04-12 10:00:12
 4    1;e;u7;2016-04-12 18:21:32
 5    1;f;u8;2016-04-13 13:27:41
 6    2;a;u2;2016-04-14 08:56:09
 7    2;b;u3;2016-04-14 09:36:02
 8    2;d;u5;2016-04-15 10:16:40
 9    1;g;u6;2016-04-18 19:14:14
10    2;g;u6;2016-04-19 15:39:15
11    1;h;u2;2016-04-19 16:48:16
12    2;e;u7;2016-04-20 14:39:45
13    2;f;u8;2016-04-22 09:16:16
14    3;a;u2;2016-04-25 08:39:24
15    2;h;u1;2016-04-26 12:19:46
16    3;b;u4;2016-04-29 10:56:14
17    3;c;u1;2016-04-30 15:41:22
```

Listing 1 shows the same event log as in Table 1, but now in CSV format. Fields are separated by semicolons, so there should be no semicolon inside a field, or else it will be interpreted as a separator.

To avoid this problem, the CSV format allows the use of text delimiters, typically a double quote (") to enclose any field that might have symbols that could be misinterpreted as a separator. However, unless the task names or user names are allowed to contain such symbols, the use of text delimiters is not very common in event logs that are used for process mining.

1.6   Reading an Event Log with Python

Reading an event log in Python is relatively simple (simpler than reading it in C, for example) since the Python language has built-in data structures such as lists, tuples, and dictionaries that facilitate most programming tasks.

The fundamental idea for reading an event log in CSV format is to open the file, read it line by line, and split each line wherever the separator symbol is found. Listing 2 shows how this can be done in Python 3.[4]

The code in Listing 2 opens the file for reading and then creates an empty list to store the events that will be read from the file. A for-loop iterates through the file, reading it line by line, until the end-of-file (EOF) is reached.

For each line fetched from the file, the first thing to do is to trim (strip) the line of any leading and trailing whitespace characters. This is being done here to remove the newline character at the end of each line.

---

[4]In most systems, the `python` command defaults to Python 2, so `python3` should be used instead.

Listing 2 Reading and printing an event log

```
1   f = open('eventlog.csv', 'r')
2
3   log = []
4
5   for line in f:
6       line = line.strip()
7       if len(line) == 0:
8           continue
9       parts = line.split(';')
10      caseid = parts[0]
11      task = parts[1]
12      user = parts[2]
13      timestamp = parts[3]
14      event = (caseid, task, user, timestamp)
15      log.append(event)
16
17  f.close()
18
19  for (caseid, task, user, timestamp) in log:
20      print(caseid, task, user, timestamp)
```

Listing 3 Output of the previous script

```
1    1 a u1 2016-04-09 17:36:47
2    1 b u3 2016-04-11 09:11:13
3    1 d u6 2016-04-12 10:00:12
4    1 e u7 2016-04-12 18:21:32
5    1 f u8 2016-04-13 13:27:41
6    2 a u2 2016-04-14 08:56:09
7    2 b u3 2016-04-14 09:36:02
8    2 d u5 2016-04-15 10:16:40
9    1 g u6 2016-04-18 19:14:14
10   2 g u6 2016-04-19 15:39:15
11   1 h u2 2016-04-19 16:48:16
12   2 e u7 2016-04-20 14:39:45
13   2 f u8 2016-04-22 09:16:16
14   3 a u2 2016-04-25 08:39:24
15   2 h u1 2016-04-26 12:19:46
16   3 b u4 2016-04-29 10:56:14
17   3 c u1 2016-04-30 15:41:22
```

If, as a result of this trimming, the line becomes empty, then this is just a blank line and we can proceed to the next line. Sometimes, there is a blank line at the end of the log file, so it is a good idea to skip it instead of attempting to parse it.

If the line is not empty, the script assumes that it will be possible to split the line into four parts that are separated by semicolon. The split() function returns a list of parts, and each of those parts is assigned to a different variable. If the event log contains additional columns, which sometimes happens in practice, then there will be some extra parts that will remain unused.

The script then creates a tuple with those variables (line 14), and appends this tuple to the list of events (line 15). After having done this for every line, the script closes the file (this is important not to forget).

Finally, just for illustrative purposes, the script iterates through the list of events and prints their contents. The output is shown in Listing 3.

For more complicated event logs with text delimiters, escape characters, different line terminators, etc., the Python language provides a built-in `csv` module[5] that can handle all those variants. The NumPy library[6] and the Pandas library[7] also have powerful routines to read CSV files, but they are more geared towards numerical applications. Anyway, this is just a matter of getting familiar with the documentation for those modules and libraries, so we leave it to the interested reader to explore further. Our main goal here is to focus on the fundamental ideas.

1.7 Sorting an Event Log with Python

Listing 3 shows that the event log is sorted by timestamp, and this is usually what happens in practice, as events are recorded sequentially in the order in which they occurred. However, for the purpose of process mining, it is often convenient to bring together all the events that belong to the same case id.

Sorting the event log must be done carefully in order to keep the relative order of events within the same case id. Consider what happens when running `log.sort()` on the list created in Listing 2. The `sort()` method will sort the events by case id and then, if two events have the same case id, it will sort them by task. As a result, we could end up with the output shown in Listing 4.

Here, the sorting has changed the order of events in case id 2. While, in Listing 3, case id 2 had the task transitions $g \to e \to f$, in Listing 4 the transitions are $e \to f \to g$ because these tasks have been brought into alphabetical order.

Clearly, we need to sort the events by case id *and timestamp* in order to keep the relative order of events within the same case id. In Python, we can do this by telling the `sort()` method which fields should be used for sorting.

The `sort()` method accepts a named argument called `key`. This `key` is a function that is called on each element of the list prior to sorting them. The idea is to use this function to do some processing on the element and return a key to be used for sorting. The elements end up being sorted by the key returned by the function instead of being sorted based on their original contents.

The syntax for doing this in Python involves a so-called *lambda function*. A lambda function is an anonymous function that has simply a list of arguments and an expression to compute its result. For example, the lambda function in Listing 5 computes the square of its argument.

Going back to our problem, we need to sort the event log by case id and timestamp. For this purpose, it is possible to use a lambda function that extracts the case id and timestamp from a given event. The case id and timestamp will be used as key for sorting. Listing 6 shows how to do this.

---

[5]https://docs.python.org/3/library/csv.html.

[6]http://www.numpy.org/.

[7]http://pandas.pydata.org/.

Listing 4 Wrong sorting of the event log by case id

```
1    1 a u1 2016-04-09 17:36:47
2    1 b u3 2016-04-11 09:11:13
3    1 d u6 2016-04-12 10:00:12
4    1 e u7 2016-04-12 18:21:32
5    1 f u8 2016-04-13 13:27:41
6    1 g u6 2016-04-18 19:14:14
7    1 h u2 2016-04-19 16:48:16
8    2 a u2 2016-04-14 08:56:09
9    2 b u3 2016-04-14 09:36:02
10   2 d u5 2016-04-15 10:16:40
11   2 e u7 2016-04-20 14:39:45
12   2 f u8 2016-04-22 09:16:16
13   2 g u6 2016-04-19 15:39:15 # this event is misplaced
14   2 h u1 2016-04-26 12:19:46
15   3 a u2 2016-04-25 08:39:24
16   3 b u4 2016-04-29 10:56:14
17   3 c u1 2016-04-30 15:41:22
```

Listing 5 A simple lambda function

```
1    f = lambda x: x**2
2    y = f(2) + f(3) # the result is 4 + 9 = 13
3    print(y)
```

Listing 6 Sorting with a lambda function

```
1    log.sort(key = lambda event: (event[0], event[-1]))
```

Listing 7 Correct sorting of the event log by case id and timestamp

```
1    1 a u1 2016-04-09 17:36:47
2    1 b u3 2016-04-11 09:11:13
3    1 d u6 2016-04-12 10:00:12
4    1 e u7 2016-04-12 18:21:32
5    1 f u8 2016-04-13 13:27:41
6    1 g u6 2016-04-18 19:14:14
7    1 h u2 2016-04-19 16:48:16
8    2 a u2 2016-04-14 08:56:09
9    2 b u3 2016-04-14 09:36:02
10   2 d u5 2016-04-15 10:16:40
11   2 g u6 2016-04-19 15:39:15
12   2 e u7 2016-04-20 14:39:45
13   2 f u8 2016-04-22 09:16:16
14   2 h u1 2016-04-26 12:19:46
15   3 a u2 2016-04-25 08:39:24
16   3 b u4 2016-04-29 10:56:14
17   3 c u1 2016-04-30 15:41:22
```

Basically, the lambda function receives an event and returns a tuple containing the case id and the timestamp from that event. Remember that an event is a 4-tuple containing a case id, task, user, and timestamp. The lambda function retrieves only the first and the last fields from that tuple, packs them into a 2-tuple, and returns this as a key to be used for sorting.

As a result of this sorting, we get the correct result shown in Listing 7. Of course, if we want to get back to the event log sorted globally by timestamp, we can use a lambda function that returns only the timestamp from each event.

1.8 Reading the Event Log as a Dictionary

Another way to bring together the events that belong to the same case id is to read the event log into a dictionary, instead of reading it into a list.

Similarly to a list, a Python dictionary is a data structure that holds a collection of items. However, instead of having each item at certain position, in a dictionary each item is associated with a certain *key*. A key and its corresponding item are usually referred to as a *key-value pair* (even though the "value" here may be a complex data structure). A dictionary is a collection of key-value pairs.

To bring together events within the same case id, the idea is to use the case id as key. Associated with that key, there will be a list of events (i.e. the item or "value" associated with the key is actually a list of events). In other words, each case id (serving here as key) will be associated with the list of events that belong to that case id. Naturally, this list of events must be sorted by timestamp.

Listing 8 shows how the events can be read into a dictionary.

The code is very similar to Listing 2 on page 8, but has the following differences:

- The `log` variable is now initialized as a `dict()` rather than as a list (`[]`).
- For each line that is read from the log file, it is necessary to check if the case id already exists in the dictionary. If it does not exist (line 14), then a new key is inserted into the dictionary (line 15). The list of events associated with this key is initially empty.
- In contrast to Listing 2, each event is now a 3-tuple with task, user, and timestamp (line 16). The event is appended to the list of events associated with the case id (line 17).

Listing 8 Reading and printing an event log with a dictionary

```
1   f = open('eventlog.csv', 'r')
2
3   log = dict()
4
5   for line in f:
6       line = line.strip()
7       if len(line) == 0:
8           continue
9       parts = line.split(';')
10      caseid = parts[0]
11      task = parts[1]
12      user = parts[2]
13      timestamp = parts[3]
14      if caseid not in log:
15          log[caseid] = []
16      event = (task, user, timestamp)
17      log[caseid].append(event)
18
19  f.close()
20
21  for caseid in log:
22      for (task, user, timestamp) in log[caseid]:
23          print(caseid, task, user, timestamp)
```

Listing 9 Output of the previous script

```
1    1 a u1 2016-04-09 17:36:47
2    1 b u3 2016-04-11 09:11:13
3    1 d u6 2016-04-12 10:00:12
4    1 e u7 2016-04-12 18:21:32
5    1 f u8 2016-04-13 13:27:41
6    1 g u6 2016-04-18 19:14:14
7    1 h u2 2016-04-19 16:48:16
8    3 a u2 2016-04-25 08:39:24
9    3 b u4 2016-04-29 10:56:14
10   3 c u1 2016-04-30 15:41:22
11   2 a u2 2016-04-14 08:56:09
12   2 b u3 2016-04-14 09:36:02
13   2 d u5 2016-04-15 10:16:40
14   2 g u6 2016-04-19 15:39:15
15   2 e u7 2016-04-20 14:39:45
16   2 f u8 2016-04-22 09:16:16
17   2 h u1 2016-04-26 12:19:46
```

Listing 10 Sorting the output by caseid and the events by timestamp

```
1    for caseid in sorted(log.keys()):
2        log[caseid].sort(key = lambda event: event[-1])
3        for (task, user, timestamp) in log[caseid]:
4            print(caseid, task, user, timestamp)
```

- When iterating through the event log, we need to go through each key (line 21) and then go through the list of events associated with that key (line 22).

The output of this script is shown in Listing 9. Note that case id 3 appears before case id 2 because, in a dictionary, keys have no particular order. However, events within the same case id appear together as desired.

If, for some reason, we would like to sort this output by case id (only the output, not the dictionary itself), then this can be done by using a list of sorted keys, as shown in Listing 10 (line 1).

For completeness, Listing 10 also includes an instruction to make sure that the list of events for each case id is sorted by timestamp (line 2). This sorting is being done in-place (i.e. by changing the list itself). The output of this code is the same as in Listing 7.

1.9   Summary

Before we proceed to the next chapter, here is a recap of the main points so far:

- Business processes are often represented as graphical models that specify the sequences of activities that are expected to be performed at run-time.
- A single process model may give origin to many process instances at run-time, with variations in their behavior and in their participants.
- Tasks are assigned to users in a non-deterministic way, depending on the conditions that are found at run-time when a process instance is being executed.

- Process mining is a means to analyze the run-time behavior of process instances, in terms of their sequence of tasks and participating users.
- Each process instance is identified by a unique case id.
- An event log is a list of recorded events, where each event contains a case id, task, user, and timestamp.
- When events logs are stored in CSV format, they can be easily parsed with the `split()` function available in Python.
- An event log can be loaded as list of events, or as a dictionary where the key is the case id and the value is the list of events associated with that case id.
- Events should be sorted by caseid and timestamp. This can be done in Python with the `sort()` method and a lambda function.

Chapter 2
Control-Flow Perspective

The control-flow perspective is a type of analysis that focuses on the discovery of the sequence of activities in a business process. The idea is that by analyzing how tasks follow each other in the event log, it should be possible to come up with a model that describes the overall behavior of the process.

There are several algorithms to discover the sequential behavior of a process, with notable examples being the *α-algorithm* [19], the *heuristics miner* [25], the *genetic miner* [9], and the *fuzzy miner* [4]. These algorithms employ different approaches to arrive at essentially the same result, which is a model that depicts the transitions between tasks.

The simplest way to do this is as follows: every time task a is followed by task b, we count that transition. We do this for all pairs of consecutive tasks within the same case id. (Transitions between tasks in different case ids do not count.) Doing this across the whole event log will provide a count of how many times each transition has occurred. Then, it is possible to combine these transitions in order to generate an output graph that captures the sequential behavior of the process.

This idea is the essence of many control-flow algorithms. Rather than looking at a range of different algorithms and their specific details, here we will focus on this single fundamental idea. Armed with a good understanding of how this idea can be implemented, the interested reader will find it easier to get acquainted with more advanced algorithms in the field of process mining.

2.1 The Transition Matrix

As stated above, we will be looking at a simple version of a control-flow algorithm. This algorithm will work with case ids and tasks. The algorithm will be described mainly in abstract terms, meaning that we will refer to examples of tasks such as

© The Author(s) 2020
D. R. Ferreira, *A Primer on Process Mining*, SpringerBriefs in Information Systems,
https://doi.org/10.1007/978-3-030-41819-9_2

a and *b* without implying a connection to the purchase process from the previous chapter. In the present context, *a*, *b*, *c*, etc., are just some arbitrary tasks.

Let us think for a moment on how we should store the information about the transitions between these tasks. Before analyzing the event log, we do not know which transitions have actually occurred, so we can only assume that any transition between those activities is possible. If we have N activities, then there are N^2 possible transitions between these activities. For example, with three activities $\{a, b, c\}$ there are nine possible transitions, namely:

$$\{a \to a, \ a \to b, \ a \to c, \ b \to a, \ b \to b, \ b \to c, \ c \to a, \ c \to b, \ c \to c\}$$

To store the count of how many times each transition has occurred, it becomes more convenient to represent these transitions in matrix form:

	a	b	c
a			
b			
c			

The nine cells in this matrix can be used to store the count of each transition. This is called the *transition matrix*. The goal of the control-flow algorithm is to go through the event log and to fill in this transition matrix with a count in each cell.

In particular, the transition matrix should be read in the following way: if in row i we find activity *a* and in column j we find activity *b*, then the cell (i, j) contains the number of times that transition $a \to b$ has been observed.

To formally describe the algorithm, it becomes more convenient to use the notation a_i for the activity in row i and a_j for the activity in column j. The activities are then $\{a_1, a_2, a_3, \ldots\}$ and the transition matrix has the following form:

	a_1	a_2	a_3	$\ldots$
a_1				
a_2				
a_3				
$\ldots$				

2.2 The Control-Flow Algorithm

Let T be the set of distinct tasks recorded in an event log, and let $|T|$ be the size of that set. For example, if $T = \{a, b, c, d, e, f, g, h\}$ then $|T| = 8$.

In mathematical terms, the transition matrix is a function $f : T \times T \to \mathbb{N}_0$ which gives the number of times that each possible transition between a pair of activities

---

Algorithm 1 Control-flow algorithm

1: Let F be a square matrix of size $|T|^2$
2: Initialize $F_{ij} \leftarrow 0$ for every position (i, j)
3: **for** each case id in the event log **do**
4:     **for** each consecutive task transition $a_i \rightarrow a_j$ in that case id **do**
5:         $F_{ij} \leftarrow F_{ij} + 1$
6:     **end for**
7: **end for**

---

in T has been observed. The objective of the control-flow algorithm is to find all the values for this function.

This can be done by initializing a transition matrix of size $|T|^2$ with zeros. As we go through the event log, every time a transition $a_i \rightarrow a_j$ is observed, we increment the value at position (i, j) in the matrix. Algorithm 1 describes this procedure.

Since the values in matrix F are obtained through a counting procedure, we will refer to those values as the *transition counts*.

2.3   Implementation in Python

There are several ways to implement the above algorithm in Python. The main decision is which data structure should be used to store the transition matrix. The matrix is bi-dimensional, so it makes sense to use a data structure that can be indexed twice (for rows and columns). With the built-in data structures available in Python, the natural choices are: a list of lists, or a dictionary of dictionaries.

Using a list of lists would involve indexing by position and it would require having a value stored at each position, even if the corresponding transition never occurs in the event log (those positions would remain with zero). This is what could be called a *dense* representation of the transition matrix.

On the other hand, using a dictionary of dictionaries allows us to index by task name and we have to introduce only the keys that correspond to the transitions that actually occur in the event log. This is what could be called a *sparse* representation of the transition matrix.

Given that the size of a full transition matrix is $|T|^2$ but probably only a subset of all possible transitions will be observed, it makes sense to use a sparse representation which avoids having to store a relatively large amount of zeros. With these issues in mind, here we will show how to implement the transition matrix as a dictionary of dictionaries.

Also, we assume that the event log has been read into a dictionary as in Listing 8 on page 11. After that, we could write the code shown in Listing 11.

At the beginning of this code, the matrix F is initialized as a dictionary. Then the script iterates through each case id in the log, and also through the list of events for that case id. Here, `ai` and `aj` are two variables that hold a pair of consecutive tasks.

Listing 11 Implementing the control-flow algorithm in Python

```
1    F = dict()
2    for caseid in log:
3        for i in range(0, len(log[caseid])-1):
4            ai = log[caseid][i][0]
5            aj = log[caseid][i+1][0]
6            if ai not in F:
7                F[ai] = dict()
8            if aj not in F[ai]:
9                F[ai][aj] = 0
10            F[ai][aj] += 1
11
12    for ai in sorted(F.keys()):
13        for aj in sorted(F[ai].keys()):
14            print(ai, '->', aj, ':', F[ai][aj])
```

Listing 12 Output of the previous script

```
1    a -> b : 3
2    b -> c : 1
3    b -> d : 2
4    d -> e : 1
5    d -> g : 1
6    e -> f : 2
7    f -> g : 1
8    f -> h : 1
9    g -> e : 1
10    g -> h : 1
```

If `ai` is not present in the matrix (line 6), then that row is initialized as a dictionary. If `aj` is not present in that row (line 8), then that position is initialized with zero. Immediately after this, and regardless of any initialization that might have been done before, the value at that position is incremented (line 10).

The rest of the script shows how to iterate through the matrix and print its contents. For every row `ai` and column `aj` (with both being sorted in alphabetical order), the script prints the value at position `F[ai][aj]`. The output of this code for the event log in Listing 1 on page 7 is shown in Listing 12.

2.4 Introducing Graphviz

Graphviz[1] is a wonderful piece of software. It can save enormous amounts of work when creating graphs, since it takes care of the graph layout automatically. Graphviz is very often used to visualize the results of process mining techniques.

To provide an idea of what Graphviz does, we will start with a simple example in Listing 13. This is a text-based definition of a directed graph. Graphviz supports both directed and undirected graphs, and this is a matter of specifying `digraph` or `graph` at the beginning of the definition.

---

[1] http://www.graphviz.org/.

Listing 13 Definition of a directed graph in Graphviz's DOT language

```
 1   digraph G {
 2       rankdir=LR;
 3       node [shape=box];
 4       a -> b [label="3"];
 5       b -> c [label="1"];
 6       b -> d [label="2"];
 7       d -> e [label="1"];
 8       d -> g [label="1"];
 9       e -> f [label="2"];
10       f -> g [label="1"];
11       f -> h [label="1"];
12       g -> e [label="1"];
13       g -> h [label="1"];
14   }
```

The graph has a name (in this case, G) and its structure comprises a series of statements enclosed in curly braces ({...}) and separated by semicolons (;). Each statement adds a piece of information to the graph definition.

The first statement rankdir=LR establishes the graph orientation from left to right (the default is TB, i.e. top to bottom). The second statement says something about the nodes in this graph. In particular, it says that the shape of nodes is a box (rectangle). Technically, shape is an *attribute* of node, and it can be specified individually for each node (in order to have nodes with different shapes, for example). However, here the shape is being specified globally for every node.

The remaining statements define the edges in the graph. It should be noted that in this example the nodes being are defined implicitly by the edges, i.e. the statement a->b defines an edge between nodes a and b and, implicitly, it also defines the nodes a and b since they have not been defined before.

Nodes and edges can also be defined separately. A common practice is to first define nodes and their attributes, and only then define the edges between those nodes. In the example of Listing 13, the edges and their attributes are being defined. In this simple example, only one edge attribute (label) is being used.

With the label attribute, we are attaching a label to each edge. A possible use for that label is to annotate the edges with the transition counts provided by the control-flow algorithm.

Generating a graph from the definition in Listing 13 is as simple as running a command such as: dot -Tpng lst13.gv -o graph.png.[2] In this command, dot is the Graphviz tool that calculates the graph layout and produces an image. Several image formats are supported, including both raster graphics (e.g. PNG, JPEG) and vector graphics (e.g. SVG).

Figure 3 shows the output generated by Graphviz. Note how Graphviz has automatically decided on the positioning of each node and has also carefully rendered the edges and their labels without any crossings or overlaps.

---

[2]To be able to run this command, you may have to install Graphviz first. In Ubuntu, Graphviz can be installed with: sudo apt-get install graphviz.

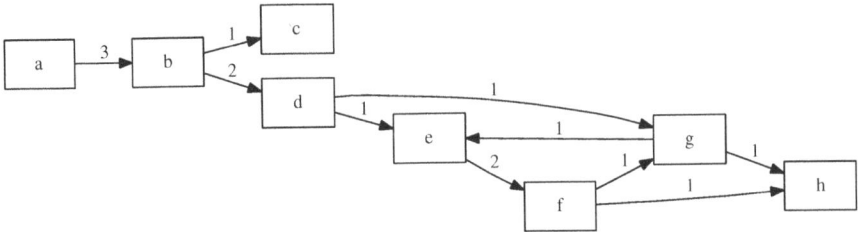

Fig. 3 Output generated by Graphviz from the definition in Listing 13

Finally, note how this graph depicts the behavior of the process shown in Fig. 1 on page 2. Naturally, this graph is not as expressive as a full-fledged process modeling language, but it certainly captures the run-time behavior of the process from the information recorded in the event log.

2.5 Using PyGraphviz

There are several ways in which one can use Python and Graphviz together. Python is a good language to implement process mining algorithms, and Graphviz is a great tool to visualize the results. The question now is how to plug these tools together in order to generate the graph from the results of the control-flow algorithm.

The simplest solution would be to modify the Python code in Listing 11 on page 18 to print the graph definition. After all, that Python script is already generating the output in Listing 12. With a few tweaks, it could as well generate the graph definition in Listing 13, which is not much different.

However, it can be a bit cumbersome to have complex graph definitions being generated with **print** instructions in Python. In addition, this would still require running dot manually in the command line in order to generate the graph.

A more elegant solution is to use a Python interface for Graphviz, such as pydot[3] or PyGraphviz.[4] Here, we use PyGraphviz which, at the time of this writing, has been in active development in recent years.[5]

Listing 14 shows how to build and generate the graph, assuming that the transition matrix has already been created by Listing 11 on page 18.

---

[3]https://pypi.python.org/pypi/pydot/.

[4]https://pypi.python.org/pypi/pygraphviz/.

[5]In order to use PyGraphviz, you may have to install it first. In Ubuntu, it can be installed with: sudo apt-get install python3-pygraphviz.

Listing 14 Generating the output graph with PyGraphviz

```
1  import pygraphviz as pgv
2
3  G = pgv.AGraph(strict=False, directed=True)
4
5  G.graph_attr['rankdir'] = 'LR'
6  G.node_attr['shape'] = 'box'
7
8  for ai in F:
9      for aj in F[ai]:
10         G.add_edge(ai, aj, label=F[ai][aj])
11
12 G.draw('graph.png', prog='dot')
```

The script starts by importing PyGraphviz and then creates a directed graph, as indicated by `directed=True`. The `strict` argument, if true, imposes certain restrictions, such as not allowing self-loops and multiple edges between the same pair of nodes. However, here we may have self-loops (i.e. transitions between the same activity), so we do not impose such restrictions.

In lines 5–6, the script sets the graph attribute `rankdir` and the node attribute `shape` in a similar way to what was done in Listing 13.

The most important part comes in lines 8–10 where the script iterates through the rows and columns in the transition matrix F and adds an edge for each transition. The edge is labeled with the transition count stored in the matrix.

Finally, in line 12 the script draws the graph by invoking the `dot` program, and saves it into an image file.

Behind the scenes, PyGraphviz generates a graph definition that is very similar to the one presented in Listing 13. The interested reader may want to try adding the instruction `print(G.string())` to the code in Listing 14 to see the graph definition generated by PyGraphviz, and compare it to Listing 13.

2.6 Edge Thickness

It often happens in practice that the event log to be analyzed is quite large and the resulting graph has a lot of edges with different transition counts, some being relatively large and others being relatively small.

By labeling each edge with the corresponding transition count, as in Fig. 3, it is possible to identify the most frequent transitions, but it still requires us to have a look at every label in order to compare those transitions and to determine, for example, which transition is the most frequent one.

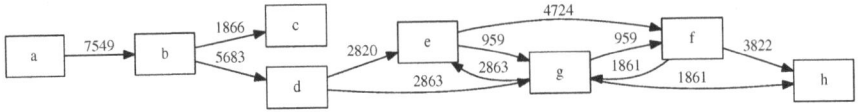

Fig. 4 Output graph generated from an event log with a large number of instances

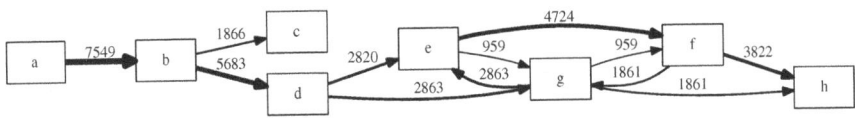

Fig. 5 Adjusting the edge thickness according to the transition count

Consider what would happen if the event log had several thousand instances. Figure 4 shows how the output graph could look like.

Here, it becomes a bit difficult to compare the transitions and determine which one is the most frequent. Of course, if we have some prior knowledge about the process, we could expect that $a \to b$ is the most frequent transition, but it would still take us a moment to confirm that in Fig. 4.

Fortunately, there is a simple way to improve the graph in order to provide a better idea of the relative frequency of transitions at first glance. This can be done by adjusting the thickness of each edge according to the corresponding transition count, as shown in Fig. 5.

A quick look at Fig. 5 suggests that $a \to b$ is the most frequent transition based on the thickness of that edge when compared to others. We can look at the transition counts to confirm this, but in any case we need to compare the labels of only the thickest edges, without having to worry about the thinner ones.

More importantly, an attentive look at Fig. 5 leads to the conclusion that the most frequent path in this process is $a \to b \to d \to g \to e \to f \to h$. This is another type of insight that can be gained by analyzing the event log.

By looking at the thickness of edges, it also becomes apparent that the number of purchase requests that are not approved (i.e. the ones that follow through activity c) is noticeably smaller than the ones which do get approved (i.e. the ones that go through activity d). From the edge labels, one can estimate that about 25% of the purchase requests do not get approved.

Edge thickness is therefore an important feature that can provide a better perception of the results of process mining techniques.

In terms of implementation, edge thickness can be controlled with the `penwidth` attribute provided by Graphviz. Basically, `penwidth` is an edge attribute just like `label`, so both of these attributes can be applied to an edge, for example as follows:
`a->b [label="3", penwidth=1.0]`.

Typically, `label` is a string (if it is a number, it will be converted to a string), but `penwidth` is a numerical value. The default value for `penwidth` is 1.0. In Fig. 4, all edges have this default value.

To produce a similar graph to that in Fig. 5, the edge thickness must be increased for those transitions which have a higher transition count. However, we do not want the edge thickness to become excessively large or excessively small. Therefore, a good practice is to define minimum and maximum values for the edge thickness, and associate them with the minimum and maximum transition counts.

Let x denote a transition count, and let y denote the corresponding edge thickness. If we want to have a linear relationship between x and y, we can use the following expression:

$$y = y_{min} + (y_{max} - y_{min}) \frac{x - x_{min}}{x_{max} - x_{min}}$$

It is easy to verify that when $x = x_{min}$ (minimum transition count), the expression yields $y = y_{min}$ (minimum edge thickness), and when $x = x_{max}$ (maximum transition count), the expression yields $y = y_{max}$ (maximum edge thickness).

Listing 15 shows how to set the edge thickness according to this expression. The differences in comparison to Listing 14 are the following:

- Line 8 puts all the transition counts in a list. A Python technique known as *list comprehension* is being used here to do this in a single line of code.
- Lines 9 and 10 compute the minimum and maximum values in that list (i.e. the minimum and maximum transition counts found in the matrix).

Listing 15 Setting the edge thickness according to the transition count

```
1   import pygraphviz as pgv
2
3   G = pgv.AGraph(strict=False, directed=True)
4
5   G.graph_attr['rankdir'] = 'LR'
6   G.node_attr['shape'] = 'box'
7
8   values = [F[ai][aj] for ai in F for aj in F[ai]]
9   x_min = min(values)
10  x_max = max(values)
11
12  y_min = 1.0
13  y_max = 5.0
14
15  for ai in F:
16      for aj in F[ai]:
17          x = F[ai][aj]
18          y = y_min + (y_max-y_min) * float(x-x_min) / float(x_max-x_min)
19          G.add_edge(ai, aj, label=x, penwidth=y)
20
21  G.draw('graph.png', prog='dot')
```

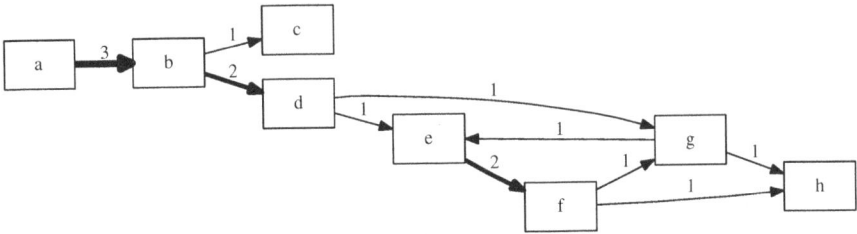

Fig. 6 Output graph generated from the previous script

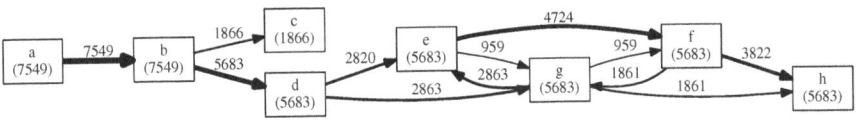

Fig. 7 Including the activity counts in each node

- Lines 12 and 13 define the minimum and maximum edge thickness, respectively.
- Line 17 stores each transition count in a variable, to be used in subsequent lines.
- Line 18 calculates the edge thickness for the given transition count (x).
- Line 19 adds an edge to the graph, now with the extra attribute `penwidth`.

The output of this code for the event log in Listing 1 on page 7 is shown in Fig. 6.

2.7 Activity Counts

In addition to transition counts, sometimes it is useful to display also activity counts, i.e. the number of times that each activity (same task name) appears in the event log. Such activity counts are also useful to identify the most common paths in the process, especially when there is a large number of transitions in the graph.

For example, consider the graph shown in Fig. 7. This is the same graph of Fig. 5, with the difference that now it includes the activity count in each node.

A quick look at this graph reveals that there are actually two groups of instances: those that end in c (1866 instances) and those that follow the other branch and end in h (5683 instances). When the graph becomes more complex, this kind of conclusion may be more difficult to reach by looking at the transition counts alone.

Therefore, it is useful to calculate the activity counts and include them in the graph. We will show how to do this in two separate listings. First, Listing 16 shows how to calculate the activity counts.

Listing 16   Calculating the activity counts

```
1   A = dict()
2   for caseid in log:
3       for i in range(0, len(log[caseid])):
4           ai = log[caseid][i][0]
5           if ai not in A:
6               A[ai] = 0
7           A[ai] += 1
```

Listing 17   Including the activity counts in the graph

```
1    import pygraphviz as pgv
2
3    G = pgv.AGraph(strict=False, directed=True)
4
5    G.graph_attr['rankdir'] = 'LR'
6    G.node_attr['shape'] = 'box'
7
8    for ai in A:
9        text = ai + '\n(' + str(A[ai]) + ')'
10       G.add_node(ai, label=text)
11
12   values = [F[ai][aj] for ai in F for aj in F[ai]]
13   x_min = min(values)
14   x_max = max(values)
15
16   y_min = 1.0
17   y_max = 5.0
18
19   for ai in F:
20       for aj in F[ai]:
21           x = F[ai][aj]
22           y = y_min + (y_max-y_min) * float(x-x_min) / float(x_max-x_min)
23           G.add_edge(ai, aj, label=x, penwidth=y)
24
25   G.draw('graph.png', prog='dot')
```

After reading the event log (see Listing 8 on page 11), we create a dictionary A to store the activity counts. A loop goes through each case id (line 2), and another loop goes through every event in that case id (lines 3). For each event, the task is stored in variable ai. If this task has not been seen before, it is inserted in the dictionary with an count of zero. Then, its count is incremented by 1.

This is a simple way to count the number of occurrences of each task. Now let us look at how to include this count in the graph. Listing 17 shows how to do this.

This is the same code as in Listing 15 except for lines 8–10. In these lines, we go through each task in the dictionary A and add a node to the graph (line 10). The node name is equal to the task name (ai). However, its label includes additional information. Specifically, the label is the result of appending the task name with the activity count inside parenthesis, and with a newline character in between (line 9).

For the event log of Listing 1 on page 7, the resulting graph is shown in Fig. 8.

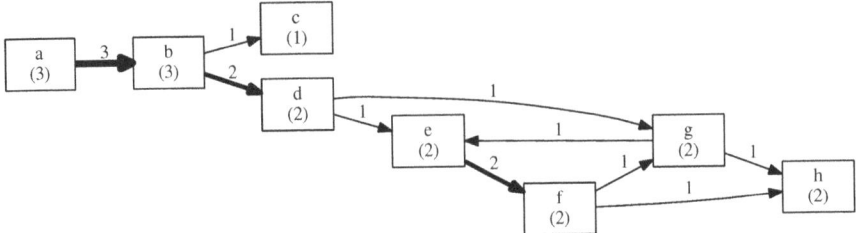

Fig. 8 Output graph generated from the previous script

It should be noted that in Listing 17 the graph is being built by first adding the nodes and only then adding the edges. Naturally, the node names that are used when adding the nodes must be the same that are used when adding the edges. The additional information about the activity counts is being included in the node labels, not in the node names.

2.8   Node Coloring

A further improvement that can be done to the graph is to color the nodes according to their activity counts. Graphviz provides an extensive set of colors, including 100 different shades of gray. This is what we will be using here. A lighter shade of gray will correspond to a lower activity count, and a darker shade of gray will correspond to a higher activity count.

To get maximum contrast, we will make the minimum activity count correspond to white, and the maximum activity count correspond to black. Any values in between will correspond to some intermediate shade of gray. With this correspondence, the graph for a large event log could look like the one in Fig. 9.

The fill color of each node now provides a visual cue of which nodes have similar activity counts. In particular, the two groups of instances mentioned in the previous section (i.e. the ones that go through activity c and the ones that go through activity d) are now easily distinguishable by their color shading.

Activities a and b have maximum shading since they have the maximum activity count. Also, note that the font color in these nodes has been changed to white in order to be readable over a dark background.

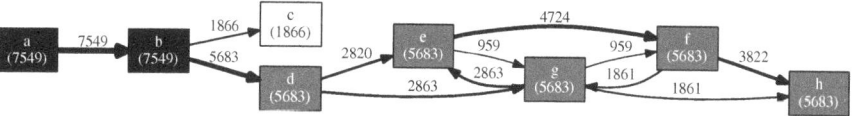

Fig. 9 Adjusting the node color according to the activity count

Listing 18 Adding fill color and setting the font color of nodes

```
1    import pygraphviz as pgv
2
3    G = pgv.AGraph(strict=False, directed=True)
4
5    G.graph_attr['rankdir'] = 'LR'
6    G.node_attr['shape'] = 'box'
7
8    x_min = min(A.values())
9    x_max = max(A.values())
10
11   for ai in A:
12       text = ai + '\n(' + str(A[ai]) + ')'
13       gray = int(float(x_max - A[ai]) / float(x_max - x_min) * 100.)
14       fill = 'gray' + str(gray)
15       font = 'black'
16       if gray < 50:
17           font = 'white'
18       G.add_node(ai, label=text, style='filled', fillcolor=fill, fontcolor=font)
19
20   values = [F[ai][aj] for ai in F for aj in F[ai]]
21   x_min = min(values)
22   x_max = max(values)
23
24   y_min = 1.0
25   y_max = 5.0
26
27   for ai in F:
28       for aj in F[ai]:
29           x = F[ai][aj]
30           y = y_min + (y_max-y_min) * float(x-x_min) / float(x_max-x_min)
31           G.add_edge(ai, aj, label=x, penwidth=y)
32
33   G.draw('graph.png', prog='dot')
```

Listing 18 shows how the graph in Fig. 9 has been generated. The new block of code is in lines 8–18.

As before, the node label includes the task name and the activity count in parenthesis (line 12). Then, according to the activity count, a gray level is chosen (line 13). In Graphviz, `gray0` corresponds to black and `gray100` corresponds to white. Therefore, we must convert the activity count into a gray level between 0 and 100, where 0 (black) corresponds to the maximum activity count, and 100 (white) corresponds to the minimum activity count.

If the activity count is denoted as x and the gray level is denoted as y, then the expression to convert an activity count to a gray level is:

$$y = \frac{x_{max} - x}{x_{max} - x_{min}} \times 100$$

It is easy to check that when the activity count is maximum ($x = x_{max}$), the expression yields 0 (black), as desired. On the other hand, if the activity count is minimum ($x = x_{min}$), the expression yields 100 (white).

The minimum and maximum activity counts have been computed before in lines 8–9. In line 13, the script applies the expression above and converts the result to an integer between 0 and 100. In line 14, the script uses this result to pick the correct shade of gray, as a Graphviz color between gray0 and gray100.

The choice of font color happens in lines 15–17. Line 15 sets the font color to the default value of black but, if the gray level is below 50 (meaning that the fill color is dark), the font color is switched to white in line 17.

Finally, the script adds the node to the graph in line 18. Several attributes are being specified: the node label, the style (to ensure that the node is actually filled), the fill color, and the font color.

2.9 Summary

Here is a brief recap of what we have learned in this chapter:

- The aim of the control-flow perspective is to extract a model of the sequence of activities from the event log. This is done by counting the transitions between successive tasks with the same case id.
- Such transition counts can be stored in a transition matrix, which is the basis for generating an output graph.
- Graphviz is a tool for drawing graphs. It takes care of the layout of nodes and edges automatically, so the minimum information required to draw a graph is a list of edges between nodes.
- Graphviz has its own language to define graphs, but there is no need to write such definitions by hand. PyGraphviz provides a convenient interface to generate such definitions from Python code.
- Both nodes and edges have attributes that can be used to improve the graph. For better visualization, edge thickness can be adjusted according to transition counts, and node color can be adjusted according to activity counts.
- Both transition counts and activity counts can be used to discover the most frequent paths (i.e. the typical behavior) in the process.

Listing 19 shows a complete script with what we have learned in this chapter.

Listing 19 Complete script for reading the event log and generating the control-flow graph

```
 1  import pygraphviz as pgv
 2
 3  f = open('eventlog.csv', 'r')
 4  log = dict()
 5  for line in f:
 6      line = line.strip()
 7      if len(line) == 0:
 8          continue
 9      [caseid, task, user, timestamp] = line.split(';')
10      if caseid not in log:
11          log[caseid] = []
12      event = (task, user, timestamp)
13      log[caseid].append(event)
14  f.close()
15
16  F = dict()
17  for caseid in log:
18      for i in range(0, len(log[caseid])-1):
19          ai = log[caseid][i][0]
20          aj = log[caseid][i+1][0]
21          if ai not in F:
22              F[ai] = dict()
23          if aj not in F[ai]:
24              F[ai][aj] = 0
25          F[ai][aj] += 1
26
27  A = dict()
28  for caseid in log:
29      for i in range(0, len(log[caseid])):
30          ai = log[caseid][i][0]
31          if ai not in A:
32              A[ai] = 0
33          A[ai] += 1
34
35  G = pgv.AGraph(strict=False, directed=True)
36  G.graph_attr['rankdir'] = 'LR'
37  G.node_attr['shape'] = 'box'
38
39  x_min = min(A.values())
40  x_max = max(A.values())
41  for ai in A:
42      text = ai + '\n(' + str(A[ai]) + ')'
43      gray = int(float(x_max - A[ai]) / float(x_max - x_min) * 100.)
44      fill = 'gray' + str(gray)
45      font = 'black'
46      if gray < 50:
47          font = 'white'
48      G.add_node(ai, label=text, style='filled', fillcolor=fill, fontcolor=font)
49
50  values = [F[ai][aj] for ai in F for aj in F[ai]]
51  x_min = min(values)
52  x_max = max(values)
53  y_min = 1.0
54  y_max = 5.0
55  for ai in F:
56      for aj in F[ai]:
57          x = F[ai][aj]
58          y = y_min + (y_max-y_min) * float(x-x_min) / float(x_max-x_min)
59          G.add_edge(ai, aj, label=x, penwidth=y)
60
61  G.draw('graph.png', prog='dot')
```

Chapter 3
Organizational Perspective

The organizational perspective includes different kinds of analysis which are related to the participants in a business process. The most common types of analysis in this perspective focus on the discovery of interactions and collaborations between users. For this purpose, the data to be analyzed are the *case id* and *user* columns in the event log.

The organizational perspective also includes techniques that combine information about users and the tasks they perform in order to derive a profile for each participant, and to discover the hierarchical structure or functional division of an organization [15]. However, here we will explore this topic only briefly. As in the previous chapter, we will focus on the core ideas, rather than delving into the full repertoire of existing techniques.

With some knowledge of the fundamental ideas and of how they can be implemented in practice, the interested reader will find it easier to get acquainted with several other variants and techniques that can be found in the literature.

3.1 Handover of Work

When people participate in a business process, they carry out their tasks and hand over the case to the next person.

If the business process is well structured (e.g. as an administrative process), the case will typically follow some predefined route across users or organizational units. On the other hand, if the process is flexible or even ad-hoc (e.g. as a technical support process), the next person to handle the case may be determined depending on the outcome of previous tasks.

In practice, it is useful to analyze the handover of work between participants in order to gain a better understanding of the business process. Such analysis provides a view of the interactions between users, and from that view it is possible to draw

© The Author(s) 2020
D. R. Ferreira, *A Primer on Process Mining*, SpringerBriefs in Information Systems,
https://doi.org/10.1007/978-3-030-41819-9_3

Algorithm 2 Handover of work

1: Let H be a square matrix of size $|U|^2$
2: Initialize $H_{ij} \leftarrow 0$ for every position (i,j)
3: **for** each case id in the event log **do**
4:     **for** each consecutive user transition $u_i \rightarrow u_j$ in that case id **do**
5:         $H_{ij} \leftarrow H_{ij} + 1$
6:     **end for**
7: **end for**

---

conclusions about the most recurring interactions, the workload that is being placed on each user, and the participants who play a central role in the process.

In the previous chapter, we have looked at a control-flow algorithm that goes through the event log and calculates the transition counts between tasks (see Algorithm 1 on page 17, and Listing 11 on page 18). For this purpose, the algorithm considered every pair of consecutive tasks within the same case id.

The same algorithm can be applied to analyze the user column in the event log (see Table 1 on page 6). By considering every pair of consecutive users with the same case id, it is possible to count how many times a given user has handed over work to another user.

Let U be the set of distinct users recorded in an event log, and let $|U|$ be the size of that set. For example, if $U = \{u_1, u_2, u_3\}$ then $|U| = 3$.

Similarly to the control-flow algorithm, here we are looking for a matrix as a function $f : U \times U \rightarrow \mathbb{N}_0$ which gives the number of times that each possible transition between users in U has been observed in the event log.

The matrix is of size $|U|^2$ and should be initialized with zeros. As we go through the event log, every time a transition $u_i \rightarrow u_j$ is observed in some case id, we increment the value at the corresponding position (i,j) in the matrix.

Algorithm 2 describes this procedure.

3.2 Implementing Handover of Work

As we did in the previous chapter, the handover-of-work matrix H can be stored as a dictionary of dictionaries, which is indexed twice by user. The implementation of Algorithm 2 is analogous to Listing 11 on page 18 where, instead of working with matrix F and tasks ai and aj, we now work with matrix H and users ui and uj.

Listing 20 shows the implementation, where the main difference to Listing 11 is in lines 4–5. Here, ui and uj represent two users. Thus, when accessing the ith event in the case id, we retrieve the user (which is at position 1 in each event tuple) rather than the task (which is at position 0).

To generate an output graph, we can use the code in Listing 21, which is essentially the same as Listing 15 on page 23, except that the node shape has been

Listing 20 Implementing the handover-of-work algorithm in Python

```
1   H = dict()
2   for caseid in log:
3       for i in range(0, len(log[caseid])-1):
4           ui = log[caseid][i][1]
5           uj = log[caseid][i+1][1]
6           if ui not in H:
7               H[ui] = dict()
8           if uj not in H[ui]:
9               H[ui][uj] = 0
10          H[ui][uj] += 1
```

Listing 21 Generating the output graph with PyGraphviz

```
1   import pygraphviz as pgv
2
3   G = pgv.AGraph(strict=False, directed=True)
4
5   G.graph_attr['rankdir'] = 'LR'
6   G.node_attr['shape'] = 'circle'
7
8   values = [H[ui][uj] for ui in H for uj in H[ui]]
9   x_min = min(values)
10  x_max = max(values)
11
12  y_min = 1.0
13  y_max = 5.0
14
15  for ui in H:
16      for uj in H[ui]:
17          x = H[ui][uj]
18          y = y_min + (y_max-y_min) * float(x-x_min) / float(x_max-x_min)
19          G.add_edge(ui, uj, label=x, penwidth=y)
20
21  G.draw('graph.png', prog='dot')
```

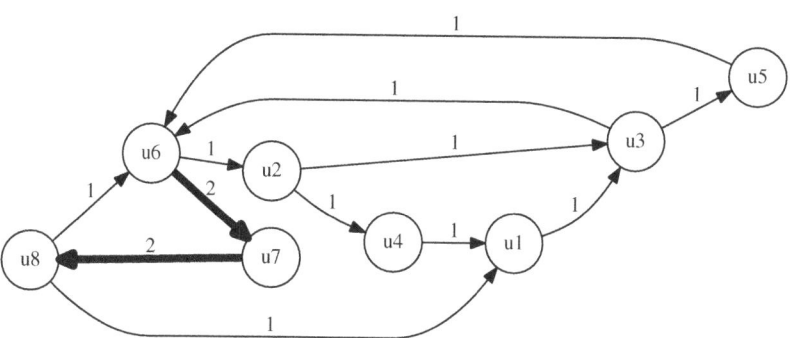

Fig. 10 Handover of work for a small event log

changed to `circle` instead of `box` (line 6). This is a useful convention to distinguish between nodes that represent users and nodes that represent tasks.

From the simple event log in Listing 1 on page 7, the generated graph is shown in Fig. 10. There is not much insight to be gained from here since the transition counts are too small.

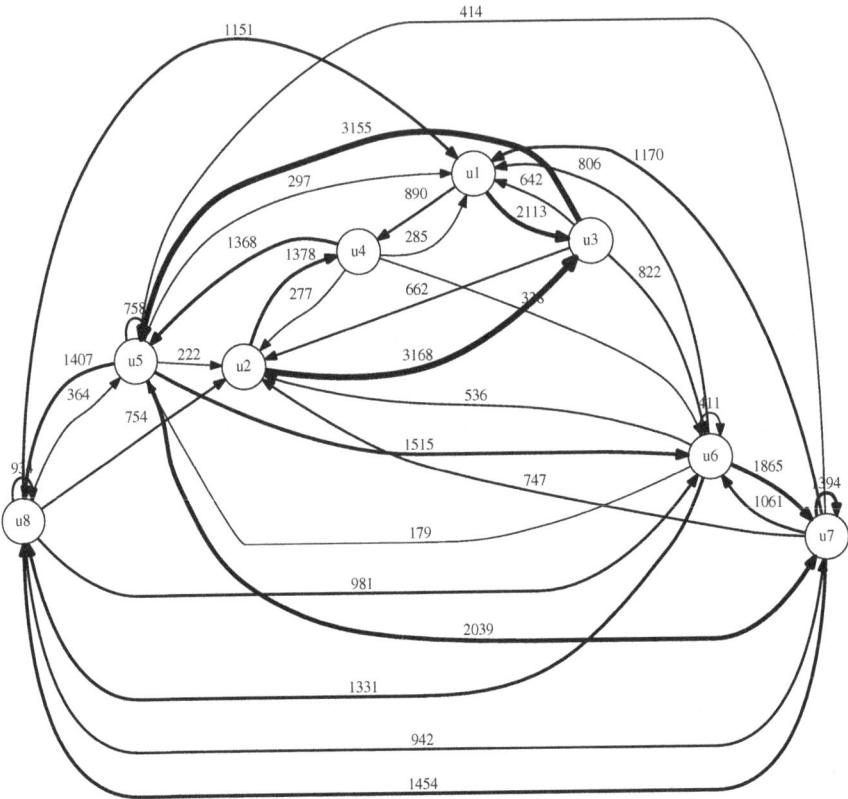

Fig. 11 Handover of work for a large event log

However, for a large event log, the graph can become significantly more complex, as shown in Fig. 11. From here, it is possible to draw some conclusions, such as the fact that a significant amount of work is being routed through user u_3.

Indeed, u_3 is one of the two managers who approve purchase requests (the other being u_4), so it is natural that this user plays a key role in the process.

3.3 Working Together

With handover of work, we can analyze the direct interactions between users as they transfer cases between them. Another interesting view is to analyze the users who participate in each case, regardless of whether they have direct interactions or not. This is useful, for example, to discover groups of users who often work together as a team in order to handle certain cases.

In particular, we want to determine, for each pair of users, how many cases those users have worked together in. For example, in the event log of Table 1 on page 6, we can see that u_1 and u_2 have worked together in all three cases.

Determining the users who have worked together (and in how many cases they have worked together) is slightly more complicated than computing the handover of work, because we must take into account both the direct and indirect interactions between users within the same case id.

As with handover of work, the goal is to arrive at a matrix that has a count for each pair of users. The difference is that here the count is the number of shared cases between those users. The matrix will have the following general form:

	u_1	u_2	u_3	...
u_1				
u_2				
u_3				
...				

To fill in the counts in this matrix, it is useful to consider the set of *distinct* users who appear in each case id. Let S denote the set of distinct users within a given case id. Then we need to go through each pair of users in S (e.g. u_i and u_j) and increment the corresponding position in the matrix.

However, in the matrix above there are actually two positions where we can store the count. There is one position that corresponds to (u_i, u_j) and there is another position that corresponds to (u_j, u_i). Since both of these positions refer to the same pair of users, we can use just one of them to store the count.

In practice, for a given set of users, it is possible to consider only those pairs in the form (u_i, u_j) where $j > i$. This results in an upper triangular matrix.

Algorithm 3 shows how the working together matrix W is computed. For each case id, the algorithm builds the set S (lines 4–7), and then a double loop goes through each pair of users in that set and increments the corresponding position in the matrix (lines 8–12).

It is interesting to compare this algorithm with Algorithm 2 on page 32. Whereas Algorithm 2 considers only direct transitions between users in a case id, Algorithm 3 considers all pairs of users from the set of users in a case id.

3.4 Implementing Working Together

The working together algorithm can be implemented in Python almost exactly as described in Algorithm 3. For this purpose, we note that Python has a built-in `set` data structure which can be used to build the set S. Listing 22 shows how to do this.

Algorithm 3 Working together

1: Let W be a square matrix of size $|U|^2$
2: Initialize $W_{ij} \leftarrow 0$ for every position (i, j)
3: **for** each case id in the event log **do**
4:     Let S be a set of users, initialize $S \leftarrow \emptyset$
5:     **for** each user u_i in the case id **do**
6:         $S \leftarrow S \cup \{u_i\}$
7:     **end for**
8:     **for** each user $u_i \in S$ **do**
9:         **for** each user $u_j \in S$ such that $j > i$ **do**
10:             $W_{ij} \leftarrow W_{ij} + 1$
11:         **end for**
12:     **end for**
13: **end for**

Listing 22 Implementing the working together algorithm

```
1   W = dict()
2   for caseid in log:
3       S = set()
4       for i in range(0, len(log[caseid])):
5           ui = log[caseid][i][1]
6           S.add(ui)
7       S = sorted(list(S))
8       for i in range(0, len(S)-1):
9           for j in range(i+1, len(S)):
10              ui = S[i]
11              uj = S[j]
12              if ui not in W:
13                  W[ui] = dict()
14              if uj not in W[ui]:
15                  W[ui][uj] = 0
16              W[ui][uj] += 1
17
18  for ui in sorted(W.keys()):
19      for uj in sorted(W[ui].keys()):
20          print(ui, '--', uj, ':', W[ui][uj])
```

Again, we assume that the event log has been read into a dictionary as in Listing 8 on page 11. The script goes through each case id in the event log (line 2) and builds the set s with all users that participate in that case id (lines 3–6).

Python guarantees that a set has no repeated elements, so we end up with the set of distinct users for each case id, which is exactly what we need for this algorithm.

In line 7, the script converts the set s to a list and then sorts its elements. This is being done to ensure that, regardless of the actual users in s, they are always considered in the same relative order (i.e. if $j > i$ then u_j appears after u_i).

In lines 8–9, the script has a double loop to go through each pair of users. Note that the second loop starts from $i + 1$. This ensures that $j > i$ and therefore we are iterating through all pairs of users (u_i, u_j) with $j > i$, as desired.

The rest of the code (lines 10–16) should be self explanatory. If there is no row for u_i in the matrix, then that row is initialized as a dictionary (lines 12–13). If u_j is not present in that row, then that position is initialized with zero (lines 14–15). After this, the value at that position is incremented (line 16).

Listing 23 Output of the previous script

```
 1    u1 -- u2 : 3
 2    u1 -- u3 : 2
 3    u1 -- u4 : 1
 4    u1 -- u5 : 1
 5    u1 -- u6 : 2
 6    u1 -- u7 : 2
 7    u1 -- u8 : 2
 8    u2 -- u3 : 2
 9    u2 -- u4 : 1
10    u2 -- u5 : 1
11    u2 -- u6 : 2
12    u2 -- u7 : 2
13    u2 -- u8 : 2
14    u3 -- u5 : 1
15    u3 -- u6 : 2
16    u3 -- u7 : 2
17    u3 -- u8 : 2
18    u5 -- u6 : 1
19    u5 -- u7 : 1
20    u5 -- u8 : 1
21    u6 -- u7 : 2
22    u6 -- u8 : 2
23    u7 -- u8 : 2
```

Finally, lines 18–20 iterate through the matrix (in sorted order of rows and columns) and print the count (i.e. the number of shared cases) for each pair of users. Listing 23 shows the output of this script for the simple event log of Listing 1 on page 7. The output confirms that u_1 and u_2 have worked together in all three cases.

3.5 Undirected Graphs

In the control-flow algorithm described in the previous chapter, and in the handover-of-work algorithm described at the beginning of this chapter, the end result was presented in the form of a directed graph (see Fig. 3 on page 20, and Fig. 10 on page 33). Those graphs depict the sequential behavior of the process that can be derived from the transitions between consecutive tasks or users in each case id.

On the other hand, the working together algorithm considers the set of users who participate in each case id, regardless of the actual order in which they appear in that case id. For this purpose, it does not matter if we say that u_1 has worked together with u_2 in three cases, or that u_2 has worked together with u_1 in three cases.

Therefore, the count of shared cases in which a pair of users have worked together can be seen as an undirected relationship between u_i and u_j, and the proper way to represent these relationships is with an undirected graph.

In Graphviz, an undirected graph is defined with the keyword `graph` instead of `digraph` (see Listing 13 on page 19). In addition, the edges in an undirected graph are defined with a double dash (`--`) rather than with an arrow (`->`).

When using PyGraphviz, changing from a directed graph to an undirected graph is a matter of changing `directed=True` to `directed=False` when creating the

Listing 24 Generating an undirected graph with PyGraphviz

```
1   import pygraphviz as pgv
2
3   G = pgv.AGraph(strict=False, directed=False)
4
5   G.graph_attr['rankdir'] = 'LR'
6   G.node_attr['shape'] = 'circle'
7
8   for ui in W:
9       for uj in W[ui]:
10          G.add_edge(ui, uj, label=W[ui][uj])
11
12  G.draw('graph.png', prog='dot')
```

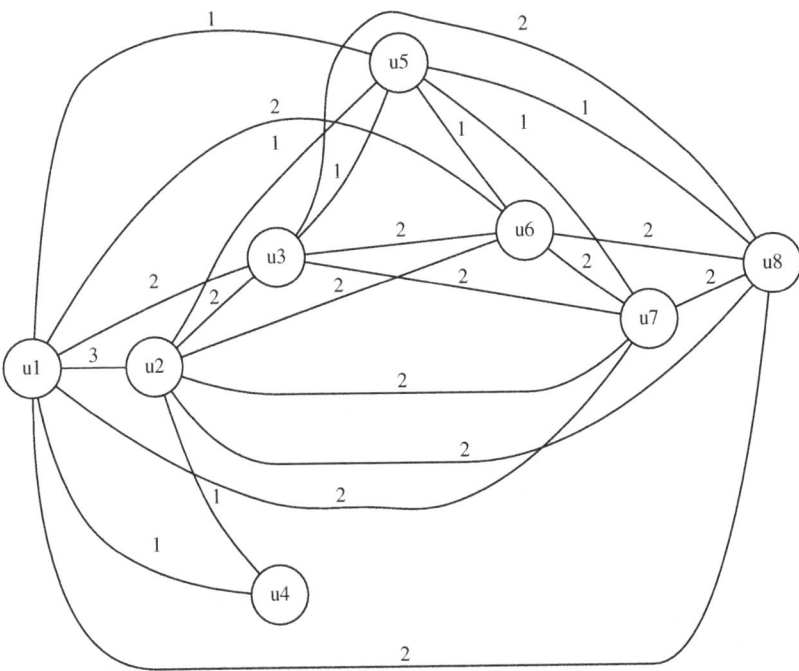

Fig. 12 Output graph generated from the previous script

graph, as shown in Listing 24 (line 3). Edges can then be added as before, with
add_edge() (line 10). PyGraphviz will know whether to create directed edges or
undirected edges depending on the kind of graph that is being used.

Figure 12 shows the graph that is generated by the working together algorithm
from the simple event log in Listing 1 on page 7.

3.6 Edge Thickness

Even for a simple event log such as the one in Listing 1 on page 7, the output graph generated by the working together algorithm can become quite complex and difficult to understand, as shown in Fig. 12.

One way to make the graph more readable is to make use of edge thickness, as we did in the previous chapter. However, rather than using a linear expression, in this kind of undirected graph the strongest relationships can be easier to visualize if we use a quadratic or even cubic expression such as:

$$y = y_{min} + (y_{max} - y_{min}) \left(\frac{x - x_{min}}{x_{max} - x_{min}} \right)^3$$

where x is the edge count and y is the corresponding edge thickness for that count.

The quantities x_{max} and x_{min} refer to the maximum and minimum values found in the matrix W, and the quantities y_{max} and y_{min} correspond to the desired limits (maximum and minimum) for the edge thickness.

Listing 25 shows how to implement this expression with the exponentiation operator (**) in Python (line 18).

Figure 13 shows the end result for a large event log, where it is easy to spot the strong relationships between (u_1, u_3), (u_2, u_3), and (u_5, u_7), for example.

These relationships are the basis for identifying clusters of users who often work together as a team. For this purpose, it is possible to use classical data mining techniques, such as *hierarchical clustering* [5], which consists in merging the nodes with the strongest links. This can be done iteratively until a desired number of clusters is reached, or until the network achieves an optimal structure according to some metric, such as *modularity* [11]. An example of the use of hierarchical

Listing 25 Setting the edge thickness according to the count of shared cases

```
 1   import pygraphviz as pgv
 2
 3   G = pgv.AGraph(strict=False, directed=False)
 4
 5   G.graph_attr['rankdir'] = 'LR'
 6   G.node_attr['shape'] = 'circle'
 7
 8   values = [W[ui][uj] for ui in W for uj in W[ui]]
 9   x_min = min(values)
10   x_max = max(values)
11
12   y_min = 1.0
13   y_max = 5.0
14
15   for ui in W:
16       for uj in W[ui]:
17           x = W[ui][uj]
18           y = y_min + (y_max-y_min) * (float(x-x_min) / float(x_max-x_min))**3
19           G.add_edge(ui, uj, label=x, penwidth=y)
20
21   G.draw('graph.png', prog='dot')
```

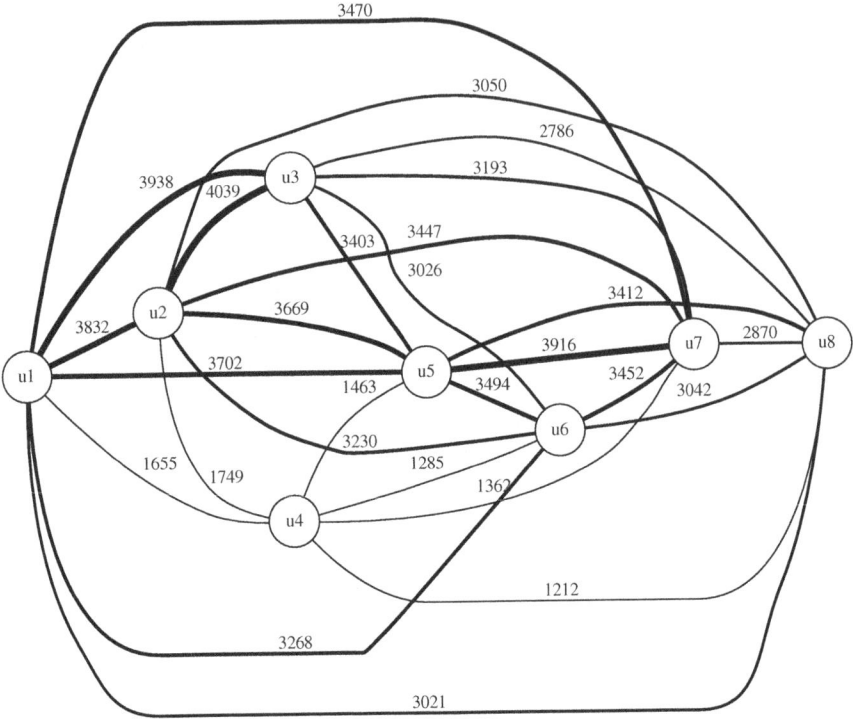

Fig. 13 Output graph generated from the previous script on a large event log

clustering to discover an organizational model can be found in [15]. An example of the use of modularity to determine the ideal number of clusters can be found in [2].

The same kind of graph can also be used to compute several metrics that are common in the field of *social network analysis* [13, 24]. Examples of such metrics are node *degree* (based on the links to other nodes), *centrality* (based on the distance to all other nodes), and *cliques* (subsets of fully connected nodes). Some of these metrics have already been used in the field of process mining [20].

3.7 Users and Activities

In the graph of Fig. 13, the links between nodes represent the number of shared cases between users. Another measure that could be used to analyze the relationships between users is the number of shared activities.

Specifically, we want to determine, for each pair of users, how many activities in common they are able to perform. For example, in the event log of Table 1 on page 6, we can see that the approval activity (task *b*) can be performed either by u_3 or u_4. This counts as one shared activity between those users (regardless of how

Listing 26 Collecting the set of activities performed by each user

```
1  UA = dict()
2  for caseid in log:
3    for i in range(0, len(log[caseid])):
4      ai = log[caseid][i][0]
5      ui = log[caseid][i][1]
6      if ui not in UA:
7        UA[ui] = set()
8      UA[ui].add(ai)
```

Listing 27 Creating a graph with the number of shared activities between users

```
1  import pygraphviz as pgv
2
3  G = pgv.AGraph(strict=False, directed=False)
4
5  G.graph_attr['rankdir'] = 'LR'
6  G.node_attr['shape'] = 'circle'
7
8  U = sorted(UA.keys())
9  for i in range(0, len(U)-1):
10   for j in range(i+1, len(U)):
11     ui = U[i]
12     uj = U[j]
13     x = len(UA[ui] & UA[uj])
14     if x > 0:
15       G.add_edge(ui, uj, label=x)
16
17 G.draw('graph.png', prog='dot')
```

many times the activity appears in the event log). The fact that either u_3 or u_4 can approve a purchase suggests that they may have similar responsibilities.

This kind of relationship between users can be gathered by going through the event log and collecting the set of activities performed by each user. We can then compare the sets of activities performed by different users. In Python, it is possible to store these sets of activities in a dictionary that is indexed by user.

Listing 26 shows how to do this. After reading the event log as in Listing 8 on page 11, we create a dictionary UA that will store the set of activities performed by each user. For each event in the event log, we collect the task and user from the event (lines 4–5). If the user is not present in the dictionary, we add it and initialize that position as an empty set (line 7). Afterwards, we add the task to that set.

After this, we can create an undirected graph as shown in Listing 27. Here, U is the set of users that can be obtained from the keys of dictionary UA (line 8). We then iterate through all pairs (u_i, u_j) with $j > i$ (lines 9–10). The shared activities between u_i and u_j are found by intersecting the sets of activities for those users, using the Python intersection operator & (line 13).

Here we are interested in the number of shared activities, so we retrieve the size (i.e. length) of that intersection. An edge is added to the graph if the number of shared activities is greater than zero (lines 14–15).

The output graph is shown in Fig. 14. This is, in fact, the output graph for a large event log, and yet it is a relatively simple graph with four separate components. This is due to the fact that each activity in the process of Fig. 1 on page 2 is always

Fig. 14 Output graph
generated from the previous
script

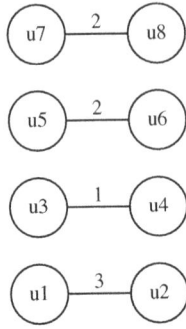

performed by one of two possible users, and the set of users who perform each activity is disjoint from other activities.

For example, activity *b* (approve request) is performed either by u_3 or u_4 and this is the single activity shared by these users in Fig. 14. On the other hand, u_7 and u_8 share two activities. It is not shown in the graph, but the two activities are *e* (receive product) and *f* (update stock). Similarly, users u_5 and u_6 share activities *d* (order product) and *g* (handle payment). Finally, users u_1 and u_2 share three activities: *a* (fill out request), *c* (archive request) and *h* (close request).

From a graph such as the one in Fig. 14, it is possible to conclude that these groups of users have clearly separate responsibilities, and therefore they probably belong to different departments or organizational units.

In practice, such divisions may not be so clear-cut. If users share activities in a flexible way, then the graph will be more interconnected and it will be necessary to use some form of clustering in order to discover the organizational structure. For a more in-depth look at this topic, the reader is referred to [15].

3.8   Work Distribution

Rather than simply gathering the set of activities that each user has performed, it is possible to actually count how many instances of each activity (i.e. how many similar tasks) were performed by each user.

This can be done with some changes to Listing 26. Basically, rather than initializing each position of the dictionary UA as a set, we initialize it as a dictionary and then use this dictionary to store a count for each activity.

Listing 28 shows how to do this. In line 7, we initialize a new dictionary for each user and, in lines 8–9, we add the activity to that dictionary if it is not already there, with an initial count of zero. Line 10 then increments the count per user and activity.

From the dictionary UA, we can now draw a graph to depict the distribution of work (i.e. the assignment activities to users) that has actually taken place during the execution of the process. Listing 29 shows how to do this.

Listing 28 Counting the number of times that each user performed each task

```
1   UA = dict()
2   for caseid in log:
3       for i in range(0, len(log[caseid])):
4           ai = log[caseid][i][0]
5           ui = log[caseid][i][1]
6           if ui not in UA:
7               UA[ui] = dict()
8           if ai not in UA[ui]:
9               UA[ui][ai] = 0
10          UA[ui][ai] += 1
```

Listing 29 Creating a graph with the counts per user and activity

```
1   import pygraphviz as pgv
2
3   G = pgv.AGraph(strict=False, directed=False)
4
5   G.graph_attr['rankdir'] = 'LR'
6   G.node_attr['shape'] = 'circle'
7
8   values = [UA[ui][ai] for ui in UA for ai in UA[ui]]
9   x_min = min(values)
10  x_max = max(values)
11
12  y_min = 1.0
13  y_max = 5.0
14
15  for ui in UA:
16      for ai in UA[ui]:
17          x = UA[ui][ai]
18          y = y_min + (y_max-y_min) * float(x-x_min) / float(x_max-x_min)
19          G.add_edge(ui, ai, label=x, penwidth=y)
20
21  G.draw('graph.png', prog='dot')
```

Basically, the code is very similar to what we have seen before. The difference is that, in this graph, each edge is a connection between a certain user and a certain activity. The edges are labeled with the count stored in dictionary UA, and the edge thickness is being set according to that count as well (lines 17–19).

As a result, this graph will have users on one side, and activities on the other side, with the correspondence between users and activities being based on the counts stored in dictionary UA. The graph for a large event log is shown in Fig. 15.

In this graph, we have four separate components as before, but now we can see the actual activities that are shared by these users, as well as the number of times that each user has performed each activity. Besides the edge label, the edge thickness is also proportional to that count.

Reading the graph in Fig. 15 from left to right shows the distribution of activities per user, which provides an idea of the proportion of effort that each user has placed on different activities.

On the other hand, reading the graph from right to left shows the distribution of users per activity, which provides an idea of how each user has contributed to the execution of each activity.

Fig. 15 Distribution of work
across users and activities

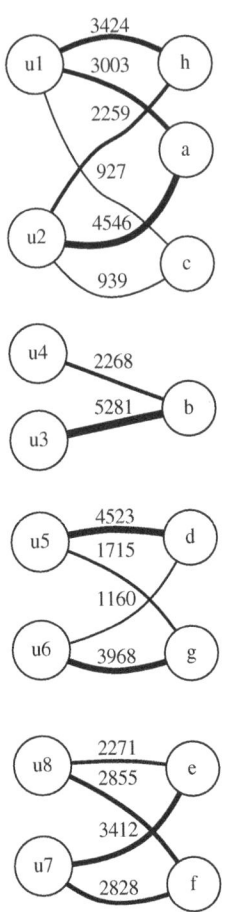

3.9   Summary

In this chapter, we have seen a series of techniques that are associated with the
organizational perspective of process mining. In particular:

- The handover-of-work algorithm is similar to the control-flow algorithm, but
  focuses instead on the sequence of users in the event log. This algorithm can
  be used to analyze the behavior of users as they transfer work between them.
- The working together algorithm focuses on the shared cases between users. It
  produces an undirected graph where the relative strength of each link provides
  an idea of how often two users have worked together on the same case.
- The graph produced by the working together algorithm can be subject to further
  analysis with hierarchical clustering and social network metrics. We have not
  delved into these possibilities, but provided pointers to the literature.

- In a similar way to what we did with control-flow graphs, the graphs produced by handover of work and working together can be enhanced with adjustable edge thickness for better visualization.
- The organizational perspective can also focus on the relationship between users and activities in order to discover different responsibilities and organizational roles among the users who participate in a process.
- The workload placed on each user and the distribution of work across a number of activities can also be analyzed within the organizational perspective.

Chapter 4
Performance Perspective

The performance perspective is concerned mainly with time. Examples of interesting time measurements are the average time it takes to perform an activity, the maximum time it takes for the process to reach a certain point, or the average end-to-end duration of each process instance.

Usually, the performance perspective is closely related to the control-flow perspective, in the sense that certain time measurements can be regarded as being associated with particular edges or paths in the control-flow graph. For this reason, it is common to start with a control-flow analysis of the event log, and only then proceed to a performance analysis. The results of the performance analysis can then be displayed over the control-flow graph.

Another approach to the performance perspective is to look at the timeline of events that occurred in each process instance. Here, the individual events are plotted in a chart along a horizontal axis that represents time. When the events from several process instances are plotted side by side, it becomes possible to compare the time at which certain activities have been performed and the relative duration of those activities or even of the entire process instances.

In this chapter, we will explore these possibilities, with the focus being placed on the main ideas. The interested reader will be able to build upon these ideas to perform more elaborate performance analysis in practice.

4.1 Dates and Times in Python

The event log in Table 1 on page 6 has a specific timestamp format. Up to now, we have been reading those timestamps simply as strings (see e.g. Listing 8 on page 11), and we have not done any special processing with them.

In the performance perspective, it is often necessary to calculate differences between timestamps. Python makes it easy to do this, provided that the timestamps

© The Author(s) 2020
D. R. Ferreira, *A Primer on Process Mining*, SpringerBriefs in Information Systems,
https://doi.org/10.1007/978-3-030-41819-9_4

Listing 30 A Python interactive session with dates and times

```
1   >>> import datetime
2   >>> ts1 = '2016-04-09 17:36:47'
3   >>> dt1 = datetime.datetime.strptime(ts1, '%Y-%m-%d %H:%M:%S')
4   >>> dt1
5   datetime.datetime(2016, 4, 9, 17, 36, 47)
6   >>> ts2 = '2016-04-11 09:11:13'
7   >>> dt2 = datetime.datetime.strptime(ts2, '%Y-%m-%d %H:%M:%S')
8   >>> dt2
9   datetime.datetime(2016, 4, 11, 9, 11, 13)
10  >>> td = dt2-dt1
11  >>> td
12  datetime.timedelta(1, 56066)
13  >>> print(td)
14  1 day, 15:34:26
```

are represented as `datetime` objects. Therefore, the first step is to parse the timestamps and convert them into that kind of object. For this purpose, we will be using the `strptime()` method that is available in the `datetime` class.

Listing 30 shows a Python interactive session that illustrates how to parse two timestamps and calculate their difference.

The script starts by importing the `datetime` module from the Python standard library, which contains the `datetime` class. The fact that the module and the class defined inside the module have the same name leads to the possibly confusing syntax of referring to the class as `datetime.datetime`.

Apart from this detail, working with the `datetime` class is relatively simple. In Listing 30, two timestamps (`ts1` and `ts2`) are being defined as strings. Then two `datetime` objects (`dt1` and `dt2`, respectively) are being created from those timestamps, with a call to the `strptime()` method of the `datetime` class.

This `strptime()` method takes two arguments: a string containing the timestamp, and another string specifying its format (lines 3 and 7).

The format is specified by means of directives, namely `%Y` for year, `%m` for month, `%d` for day, `%H` for hour, `%M` for minute, and `%S` for second.[1] There are additional directives for other details (such as time zone, week day, etc.), which may be useful in practice. The interested reader is referred to the documentation of the `datetime` module in the Python standard library.[2]

Trying to access the `datetime` objects directly reveals that these objects (`dt1` and `dt2`) are indeed instances of the `datetime.datetime` class, with multiple parts that define a certain date and time (lines 5 and 9).

Now, an interesting operation is being done in line 10, where we simply subtract the two timestamps to calculate their difference. The result is a `timedelta` object that is also defined in the `datetime` module.

Internally, the `timedelta` object is storing a duration in terms of a number of days and a number of seconds (line 12). If we print the `timedelta` object (line 13),

---

[1] Note the use of uppercase `%M` for minute and lowercase `%m` for month.

[2] https://docs.python.org/3/library/datetime.html.

the duration is converted to a human-readable string. Indeed, it is possible to verify that 56066 s correspond to 15 h, 34 min, and 26 s.

Using Python, it is possible to calculate the difference between timestamps in a simple and accurate way, without having to worry about details such as how many days has each month, or whether it is a leap year or not. This becomes very useful in the performance perspective, as we will see below.

4.2 Parsing the Timestamps

Since a timestamp can be parsed with strptime(), we will revise Listing 8 on page 11 to convert all timestamps in the event log to datetime objects. Listing 31 shows how to do this.

The differences to Listing 8 on page 11 are in line 1, where the datetime module is imported, and in line 15, where we convert the timestamp into a datetime object. The rest of the code is exactly the same, and even the double loop at the end (to print the events) needs no change because, when printing a datetime object, it is automatically converted into a string representation.

Coincidentally, this string representation happens to be in the same format as the original timestamp (i.e. %Y-%m-%d %H:%M:%S), so the output of this script is exactly the same as in Listing 9 on page 12. The difference is that, internally, the timestamps are now being stored as datetime objects rather than strings.

Listing 31 Parsing the timestamps when reading the event log

```
1   import datetime
2
3   f = open('eventlog.csv', 'r')
4
5   log = dict()
6
7   for line in f:
8       line = line.strip()
9       if len(line) == 0:
10          continue
11      parts = line.split(';')
12      caseid = parts[0]
13      task = parts[1]
14      user = parts[2]
15      timestamp = datetime.datetime.strptime(parts[3], '%Y-%m-%d %H:%M:%S')
16      if caseid not in log:
17          log[caseid] = []
18      event = (task, user, timestamp)
19      log[caseid].append(event)
20
21  f.close()
22
23  for caseid in log:
24      for (task, user, timestamp) in log[caseid]:
25          print(caseid, task, user, timestamp)
```

4.3   Average Timestamp Difference

In Fig. 6 on page 24, we have decorated each edge in the control-flow graph with
a transition count between activities. In the performance perspective, something
similar can be done by decorating each edge with the average timestamp difference
for that particular transition.

For example, if the transition $a \rightarrow b$ appears in the event log, we can subtract
the timestamps of the two events in order to get their timestamp difference. Now,
if the transition $a \rightarrow b$ occurs multiple times in the event log, we can collect all the
timestamp differences from those occurrences and then compute their average. This
will give the average timestamp difference for that particular transition.

The same can be done for every other transition. In fact, the timestamps
differences for every transition can be collected with a single pass through the
event log. In the end, it is just a matter of computing the average of the timestamp
differences that have been collected for each transition.

For convenience, the timestamp differences for each transition can be stored in a
dictionary D which, in a similar way to dictionary F in the control-flow perspective,
will be indexed twice by activity. Each position in dictionary D will store a list
of timestamp differences. In the end, the average timestamp difference can be
calculated from that list. Listing 32 shows how to do this.

The script begins by creating the dictionary D, and then iterates through each case
id in the event log. For each pair of consecutive events, it retrieves the task and the
timestamp, while ignoring the user (through the use of an underscore in lines 4–5).

If the two activities are not present in the dictionary, the script initializes
the corresponding position with an empty list (lines 6–9). Regardless of such
initialization, the script then appends the timestamp difference to the list (line 10).

Listing 32 Calculating the average timestamp difference for each transition

```
1   D = dict()
2   for caseid in log:
3       for i in range(0, len(log[caseid])-1):
4           (ai, _, ti) = log[caseid][i]
5           (aj, _, tj) = log[caseid][i+1]
6           if ai not in D:
7               D[ai] = dict()
8           if aj not in D[ai]:
9               D[ai][aj] = []
10          D[ai][aj].append(tj-ti)
11
12  for ai in sorted(D.keys()):
13      for aj in sorted(D[ai].keys()):
14          sum_td = sum(D[ai][aj], datetime.timedelta(0))
15          count_td = len(D[ai][aj])
16          avg_td = sum_td/count_td
17          avg_td -= datetime.timedelta(microseconds=avg_td.microseconds)
18          D[ai][aj] = avg_td
19          print(ai, '->', aj, ':', D[ai][aj])
```

Listing 33 Output of the previous script

```
1   a -> b : 1 day, 22:10:23
2   b -> c : 1 day, 4:45:08
3   b -> d : 1 day, 0:44:48
4   d -> e : 8:21:20
5   d -> g : 4 days, 5:22:35
6   e -> f : 1 day, 6:51:20
7   f -> g : 5 days, 5:46:33
8   f -> h : 4 days, 3:03:30
9   g -> e : 23:00:30
10  g -> h : 21:34:02
```

In a second part (lines 12–19), the script calculates the average timestamp difference for each transition. Basically, this average is being calculated by summing the timestamp differences and dividing by their count.

When summing the timestamp differences (line 14), it is important to start with an initial value of zero, and this value should be in the form of a `timedelta` object. Otherwise, Python may try to add a `timedelta` with an integer, which does not work. Hence, we use `datetime.timedelta(0)` as an initial value for the sum.

The count of timestamp differences can be obtained by simply taking the length of the list (line 15). The average timestamp difference can then be calculated by dividing the sum (a `timedelta` object) by that count (line 16).[3]

As a result of this division, the average timestamp difference may have a number of seconds with some decimal places. In fact, a `timedelta` object can store a duration down to the microseconds, which can be useful in some practical applications, but here we do not need such resolution.

Therefore, we remove those decimal places by subtracting the microseconds from the result. For this purpose, we use a `timedelta` object whose duration is just the microseconds that we intend to subtract (line 17).

The script then stores the average timestamp difference at the same position in dictionary D, effectively overwriting the contents at that position, which previously contained the list of timestamp differences (line 18).

Finally, the script prints the transition together with its average timestamp difference (line 19). The output can be seen in Listing 33. The result appears as a nicely formatted string with a number of days, hours, minutes, and seconds.

In practice, it may be interesting to calculate also the minimum, maximum, and even the standard deviation of the timestamp differences. We leave this as an exercise to the interested reader. As a hint, we note that dictionary D may end up storing multiple metrics calculated from the list of timestamp differences.

---

[3]The attentive reader will have noticed that while adding a `timedelta` with an integer does not work, dividing a `timedelta` by an integer does indeed work.

4.4 Drawing the Graph

After the code in Listing 32, we have a dictionary D that contains the average timestamp difference for each transition. Now it becomes possible to draw a graph with those average timestamp differences.

In principle, such graph can be drawn in a very similar way to what has been done before, for example in Listing 15 on page 23. However, since we are now working with average timestamp differences stored in the form of timedelta objects, some details must be handled with care.

Namely, if edge thickness is to be adjusted proportionally to the average timestamp difference, then it will be necessary to convert that timedelta object into a single number x that can be used for calculating the edge thickness y according to the following expression:

$$y = y_{min} + (y_{max} - y_{min}) \frac{x - x_{min}}{x_{max} - x_{min}}$$

Since a timedelta object contains a certain number of days and seconds, the easiest way to convert it into a single number is to calculate the total number of seconds as follows: (number of days) $\times$ 24 $\times$ 3600 + (number of seconds).

In fact, the timedelta class already includes a method called total_seconds() to perform precisely this kind of calculation. The advantage of using this method is that it takes into account also the microseconds part, if present.

Using the total_seconds() method, we can draw the graph and adjust the edge thickness according to what is shown in Listing 34.

In line 8, the list values contains all the average timestamp differences converted into a total number of seconds. From these, we extract the minimum and maximum

Listing 34 Drawing the graph with average timestamp differences

```
1  import pygraphviz as pgv
2
3  G = pgv.AGraph(strict=False, directed=True)
4
5  G.graph_attr['rankdir'] = 'TB'
6  G.node_attr['shape'] = 'box'
7
8  values = [D[ai][aj].total_seconds() for ai in D for aj in D[ai]]
9  x_min = min(values)
10 x_max = max(values)
11
12 y_min = 1.0
13 y_max = 5.0
14
15 for ai in D:
16     for aj in D[ai]:
17         x = D[ai][aj].total_seconds()
18         y = y_min + (y_max-y_min) * float(x-x_min) / float(x_max-x_min)
19         G.add_edge(ai, aj, label=D[ai][aj], penwidth=y)
20
21 G.draw('graph.png', prog='dot')
```

values in lines 9–10. On the other hand, the minimum and maximum values for the edge thickness are being defined in lines 12–13.

Then lines 15–16 iterate through each transition in dictionary D, and line 17 uses `total_seconds()` again to get a number x that can be used to calculate the edge thickness y according to the expression in line 18.

Line 19 adds an edge to the graph. Note that while `penwidth` is being set to y, the `label` is being assigned the original `timedelta` object. This object will be converted into a string representation, in the same way as it happened before when we printed it in Listing 32 and it appeared as a string in Listing 33.

The resulting graph is shown in Fig. 16. For convenience, this graph has been drawn from top to bottom (TB), as specified in line 5 of Listing 34.

Since this graph is based on only a very few cases (the ones shown in Table 1 on page 6), it is not advisable to draw too many conclusions. Nevertheless, the graph does seem to suggest that activity g (*handle payment*) might be one of the longest

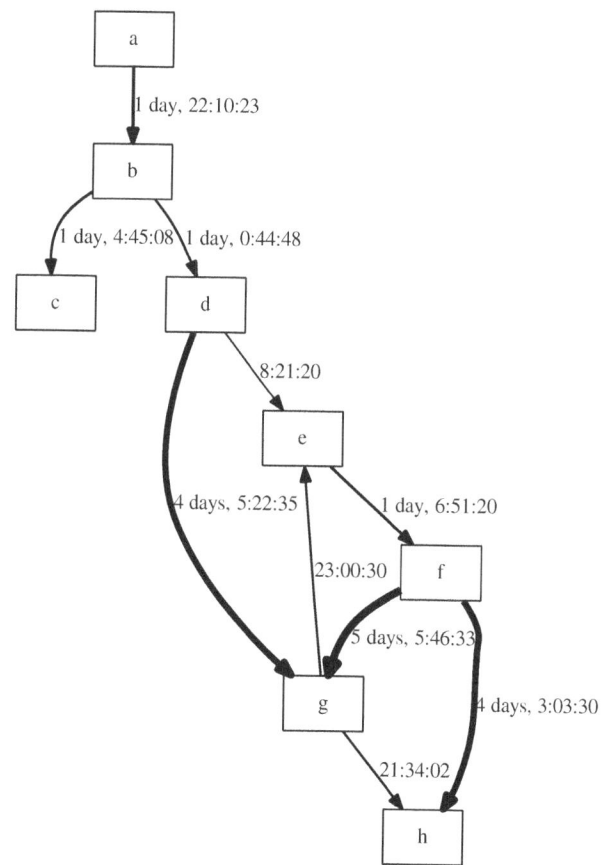

Fig. 16 Output graph generated from the previous script

in this process. This fact can be confirmed by carrying out the same analysis on a larger event log.

4.5 Analyzing the Timeline of Events

In the previous section, we have been working with average timestamp differences, which is as way to produce aggregate results from many process instances. However, in the performance perspective it is often useful to have a look at the individual events in order to analyze the timeline of events in each process instance.

Figure 17 shows a dot plot of events, also referred to as a *dotted chart* in the process mining literature [14]. In this plot, the horizontal axis represents time, and the vertical axis separates the different case ids that appear in the event log.

Within a case id, the events are usually represented with different colors, depending on the particular activity that has been performed. The same colors are reused in other case ids to denote the same activities. This way it becomes possible to pinpoint every occurrence of some particular activity across the chart.

When some of these occurrences are vertically aligned, this means that the same activity has been performed across multiple process instances at the same time, or on the same date. This is usually indicative that there may have been some fixed deadline in the process, or some batch processing on multiple cases at once.

Looking at the sequence of colors in the dotted chart can also provide interesting insights. The same sequence of colors in different case ids suggests that those

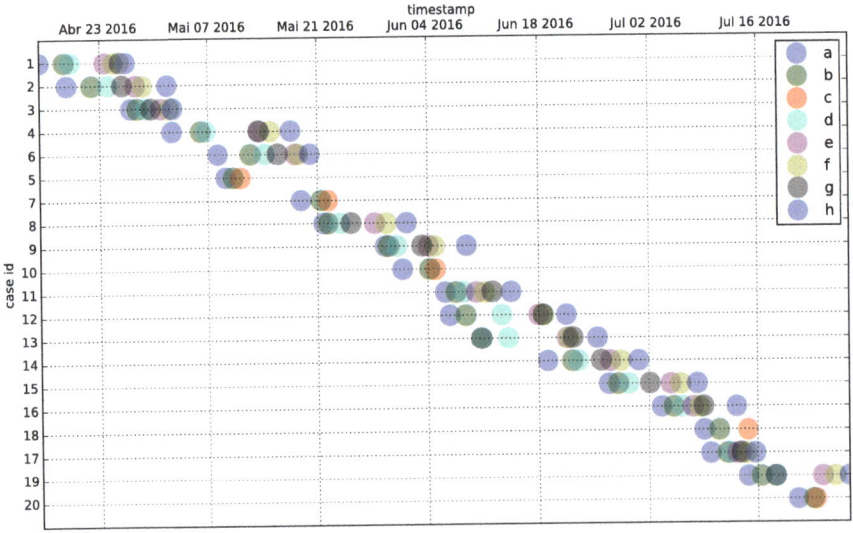

Fig. 17 Timeline of events for the first 20 instances of a large event log

instances have similar behavior, while sequences of colors that are visually distinct point to different behaviors.

Sometimes, just by looking at the number of dots in each case id it is possible to distinguish between different behaviors. For example, in Fig. 17 some instances have just three dots, while most other instances have seven events.

Depending on the dot size and the time frame being displayed, some dots may overlap and even hide other events. This is why we have used some transparency in Fig. 17 to make such overlaps more visible. However, this transparency has the disadvantage of apparently creating new colors when those overlaps occur.

More importantly, the dotted chart can be very useful to identify process instances which have suffered significant delays. The spacing between two dots gives an idea of how long it took to perform some activity. An excessive space between dots may point to inefficiencies or unexpected delays.

In general, any efficiency improvement should focus on the activities which are the most time-consuming. The dotted chart provides a convenient way to identify those activities, and also some patterns of behavior as described in [8].

4.6 Plotting the Dotted Chart

The dotted chart in Fig. 17 was created with Matplotlib,[4] a plotting library for Python. Matplotlib is the basis for much of the scientific visualization that is done with Python, and is often used together with libraries such as NumPy[5] and SciPy.[6]

Matplotlib is a generic plotting library. While it does have built-in support for some special kinds of plots (e.g. histograms, bar charts, contour plots, etc.), it does not have any particular support for dotted charts. However, these can be generated using the generic plotting routines of Matplotlib.

The approach that we describe here is meant for illustrative purposes only. It will work on small event logs with tens or a few hundred instances, but perhaps not on larger event logs with thousands of instances. In any case, it will serve to illustrate that it is not very difficult to generate a dotted chart in Matplotlib or, for that matter, any other plotting library. It just happens that Matplotlib fits well with the Python scripts that we have been looking at so far.

Listing 35 shows how the dotted chart can be plotted with Matplotlib. The main idea is to build the dotted chart as a combination of multiple plots in the same figure. Each call to the plot() function (lines 19–20) will draw the dots for a particular activity, and these dots will all be drawn with the same color.

The actual data points are stored in dictionaries x and y. These dictionaries are indexed by task. For a given task a, dictionary x will contain the timestamps of every

---

[4]http://matplotlib.org/.

[5]http://www.numpy.org/.

[6]https://www.scipy.org/.

Listing 35 Plotting a dotted chart with Matplotlib

```
1   import matplotlib.pyplot as plt
2
3   X = dict()
4   Y = dict()
5
6   caseids = sorted(log.keys(),
7                    key=lambda caseid: log[caseid][0][-1])
8
9   for (y, caseid) in enumerate(caseids):
10     for i in range(0, len(log[caseid])):
11        (a, _, x) = log[caseid][i]
12        if a not in X:
13           X[a] = []
14           Y[a] = []
15        X[a].append(x)
16        Y[a].append(y)
17
18  for a in sorted(X.keys()):
19     plt.plot(X[a], Y[a], 'o', label=a,
20              markersize=20, markeredgewidth=0., alpha=0.5)
21
22  axes = plt.gca()
23
24  axes.set_yticks(range(len(caseids)))
25  axes.set_ylim(-1, len(caseids))
26  axes.set_yticklabels(caseids)
27  axes.set_ylabel('case id')
28  axes.invert_yaxis()
29
30  axes.set_xlabel('timestamp')
31  axes.xaxis.tick_top()
32  axes.xaxis.set_label_position('top')
33
34  plt.grid(True)
35  plt.legend(numpoints=1)
36  plt.tight_layout()
37  plt.show()
```

occurrence of a, and dictionary Y will contain the case ids that correspond to those occurrences. Plotting X[a] versus Y[a] will then draw all the dots for a.

In more detail, lines 3–4 create the dictionaries X and Y. Then lines 6–7 get the list of case ids sorted by the timestamp of their first event. Sorting the case ids in this way is important so that, as we move down in the dotted chart, we always see case ids that begin later than the previous ones.

Recall that, according to Listing 31 on page 49, the event log is stored as a dictionary that is indexed by case id. The lambda function in line 7 of Listing 35 gets, for each case id, the first event in that case id (log[caseid][0]) and then the last field in that event tuple (log[caseid][0][-1]), which is the timestamp.

In line 9, we go through each case id in the sorted list of case ids. However, these case ids may be any kind of identifier, possibly strings. Therefore, we enumerate them, i.e. besides the case id we also get y as the position of that case id in the sorted list. This position y goes from 0 to $n-1$, where n is the length of the list.

Lines 10–16 then go through each event in the case id, retrieving the task (a) and the timestamp (x). The timestamp is appended to X[a], and the case id (actually, its position y in the sorted list of case ids) is appended to Y[a].

Lines 18–20 just go through each task a (in sorted order) and plot the dots for each task. The line style 'o' specifies that the marker for each data point should be a dot. The property markersize sets the size of the marker, and the property markeredgewith is set to zero so that the marker has no border.

The alpha property sets the color transparency. The actual color is chosen automatically by Matplotlib with each new call to the plot() function.[7]

The label property in line 19 sets the text to be used in the legend, as shown in the top-right corner of Fig. 17. Each plot is being labeled with the task name.

The rest of the script (lines 22–37) is basically concerned with configuring the axes and displaying the figure. In line 22, the function gca() gets a reference to the current axes (an Axes object in Matplotlib). Lines 24–28 set the properties of the y-axis, and lines 30–32 set the properties of the x-axis. Specifically:

- Line 24 sets a tick in the y-axis for each value of y. Line 25 sets the axis limits so that there is some space before the first value of y and also after the last value of y. Line 26 replaces the y-axis labels, so that we have the actual case ids instead of the values of y. Line 27 gives a title to the y-axis, and line 28 inverts the y-axis so that the case ids are displayed from top to bottom.
- Line 30 gives a title to the x-axis. Line 31 moves the x-axis to the top of the figure, and line 32 moves the axis title to that position as well.
- Line 34 turns on the grid, which draws vertical and horizontal lines for each tick in the x-axis and y-axis, respectively. Line 35 makes the legend appear, with a single marker for each label. Line 36 rearranges the plot so that it occupies most of the figure and reduces the unused margins as much as possible. Finally, line 37 shows (i.e. it opens) the figure with the plot.

It is interesting to note that the x-axis in the plot (Fig. 17) is a date/time axis. Indeed, in Listing 35, x is a datetime object (it corresponds to the timestamp variable in Listing 31 on page 49), and x[a] is a list of datetime objects. Yet, this required no special processing, because Matplotlib handles datetime objects by converting them to floating point numbers behind the scenes.

4.7   Using Relative Time

For the purpose of comparing the duration of process instances and to identify those which may have suffered significant delays, it is useful to plot all case ids from the same starting point rather than from their actual start time.

In other words, instead of using absolute time as in Fig. 17, it is often useful to draw the dotted chart using relative time, where dots are placed according to the

---

[7]For the interested reader, these colors can be customized by defining the *color cycle* to be used by the plot() function. See: http://matplotlib.org/examples/color/color_cycle_demo.html.

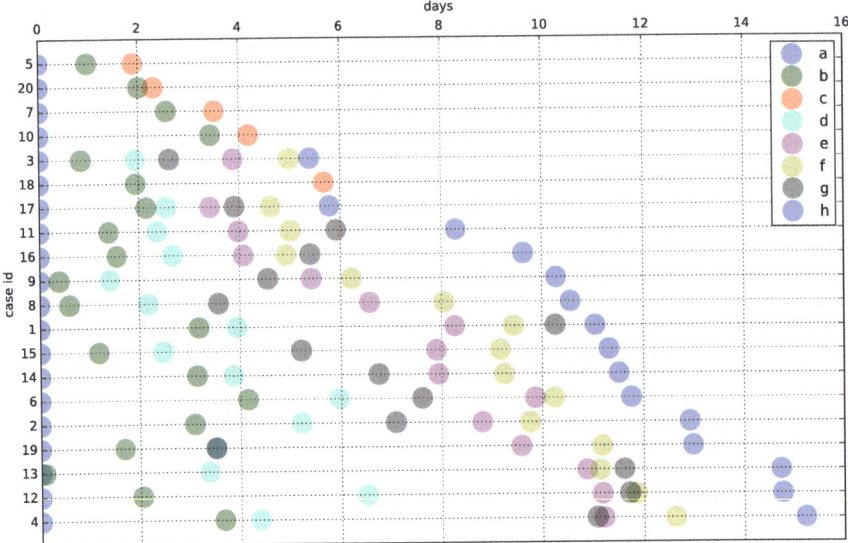

Fig. 18 Timeline of events for the first 20 instances of a large event log, using relative time

elapsed time since the first timestamp of the respective case id (i.e. time is relative to the first timestamp of the case id).

Figure 18 shows how the dotted chart would look like if plotted using relative time. The starting point (at the origin of the x-axis) corresponds to the first timestamp of each case id. The remaining dots are placed according to the time elapsed after that first timestamp. Here, the elapsed time is being measured in days.

For better visualization, the case ids have been sorted according to their end-to-end duration. The shorter instances are displayed at the top, and the longer instances are displayed at the bottom of the chart. As before, the y-axis labels display the actual case ids, but these are now in a different order than in Fig. 17.

In Fig. 18, it is possible to see that the case ids with fewer events tend to be the shortest ones. However, this is not always the case. For example, case 18 has just three events, but it is longer than case 3 with seven events. Comparing case 18 to case 20, it appears that activity c took a long time to execute in the former.

Also, the fact that some activities are carried out very quickly does not mean that the process instance, as a whole, will end much earlier. An example can be seen in case 13, where activity b is carried out almost instantaneously, but nevertheless this instance is one of the longest in the chart. This particular case id seems to have a very long time between activities d and e.

This kind of analysis is easier to perform using relative time rather than absolute time. Changing the dotted chart to relative time is not very difficult, but it requires working with timestamp differences rather than the actual timestamps.

Previously, we have seen that the difference between two `datetime` objects is a `timedelta` object with a certain number of days and seconds. We have also seen that a `timedelta` object can be converted into a single number with a call to the `total_seconds()` method. The idea is to use this method to compute the relative time that will be plotted in the dotted chart.

The dotted chart in Fig. 18 can be created with a few but important changes to Listing 35. First, the case ids need to be sorted according to their duration. Then, we need to keep track of the first timestamp of each case id in order to calculate the elapsed time for each event. Finally, we need convert that elapsed time into the desired units for display in the dotted chart.

Listing 36 shows how these changes can be implemented.

In line 7, the lambda function has been changed to calculate the difference between the timestamp of the last event and the timestamp of the first event in a case id. Therefore, case ids will be sorted based on this difference.

In line 10, the variable x0 holds the first timestamp of the case id. This is then used to calculate the timestamp difference (x-x0) in line 16.

Listing 36 Plotting a dotted chart with relative time

```
1   import matplotlib.pyplot as plt
2
3   X = dict()
4   Y = dict()
5
6   caseids = sorted(log.keys(),
7                    key=lambda caseid: log[caseid][-1][-1]-log[caseid][0][-1])
8
9   for (y, caseid) in enumerate(caseids):
10      x0 = log[caseid][0][-1]
11      for i in range(0, len(log[caseid])):
12          (a, _, x) = log[caseid][i]
13          if a not in X:
14              X[a] = []
15              Y[a] = []
16          X[a].append((x-x0).total_seconds()/(24*3600))
17          Y[a].append(y)
18
19  for a in sorted(X.keys()):
20      plt.plot(X[a], Y[a], 'o', label=a,
21               markersize=20, markeredgewidth=0., alpha=0.5)
22
23  axes = plt.gca()
24
25  axes.set_yticks(range(len(caseids)))
26  axes.set_ylim(-1, len(caseids))
27  axes.set_yticklabels(caseids)
28  axes.set_ylabel('case id')
29  axes.invert_yaxis()
30
31  axes.set_xlabel('days')
32  axes.xaxis.tick_top()
33  axes.xaxis.set_label_position('top')
34
35  plt.grid(True)
36  plt.legend(numpoints=1)
37  plt.tight_layout()
38  plt.show()
```

This timestamp difference is a `timedelta` object which is converted into a total number of seconds with a call to the `total_seconds()` method. This total number of seconds is then divided by 24×3600 to give a number of days.

Finally, in line 31 we set the title of the x-axis accordingly.

4.8 Activity Duration

A natural question in the performance perspective is to ask how long it takes to perform each activity. Despite being a simple question, it may be difficult to provide an accurate answer based on the information contained in the event log.

For example, in the event log of Table 1 on page 6, each event records the moment when a certain task has completed, but we do not know exactly when each task has started. If we suppose that each task has started after the previous one has completed, we are assuming a sequential flow of activities. This is not always the case, as can be seen from the parallel branches in Fig. 1 on page 2.

In that process, if activity g completes between e and f, it may appear that g was performed after e when in fact it was performed d. If we take the timestamp difference between e and g to measure the duration of g, we are actually underestimating it, because we should take the timestamp difference between d and g.

This is another reason for carrying out a control-flow analysis before turning to the performance perspective. Nevertheless, it may be useful to provisionally assume that all tasks took place in a linear, sequential flow, and to use the timestamp difference between consecutive events as a rough indicator of task duration.

Under this assumption, the duration of each task can be measured as the elapsed time since the previous event in the same case id.

In general, for a given activity, there will be multiple measurements for its duration, one for each occurrence of the activity in the event log. In the end, it is possible to calculate the average of those measurements. Here, we will be looking at the distribution of those measurements in order to get a sense of how long an activity typically lasts, and also how much variability we can find in such duration.

Figure 19 shows a histogram of the measurements of activity duration collected from a large event log. For some activities, the histogram is strikingly similar to a normal distribution with a certain mean and standard deviation.

For example, the duration of activity b has a mean of about 2 days and a standard deviation of about 1 day, which is roughly the same as activity h.[8]

Activities c, d and f are somewhat shorter, but even for those activities there is a long tail in the distribution, meaning that there are some instances where these activities take a long time (i.e. several days) to complete.

---

[8]Recall that the standard deviation is the distance from the mean which spans (on both sides of the mean) about 68% of data.

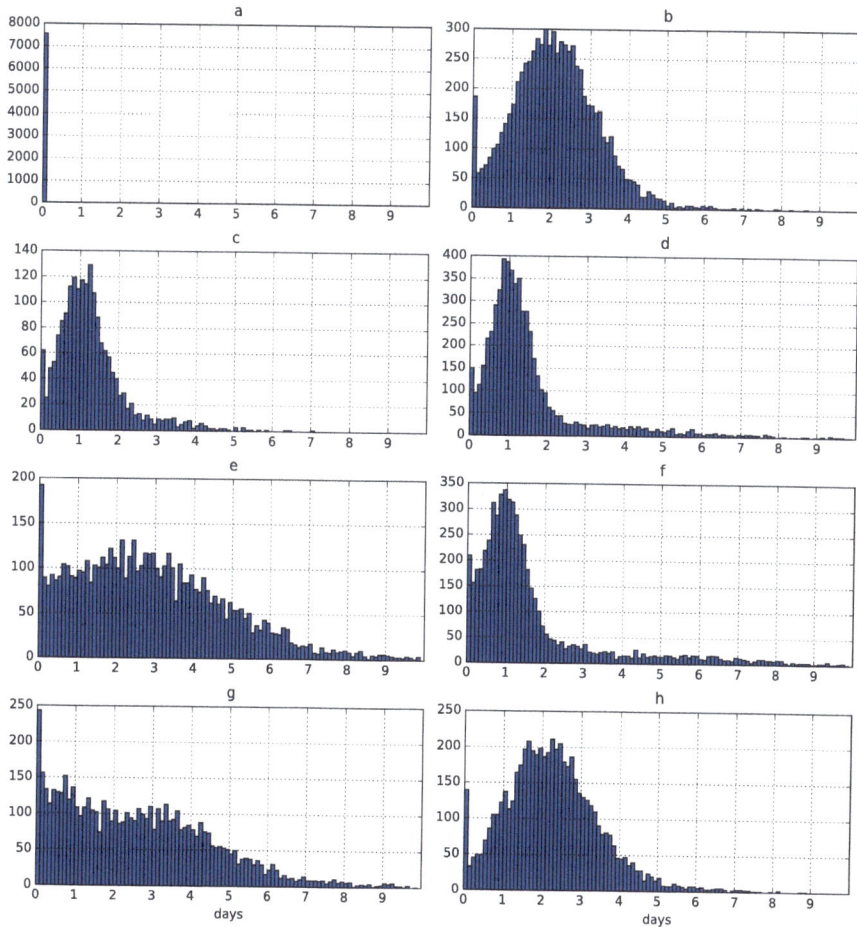

Fig. 19 Histograms of activity duration for a large event log

The histogram for *e* and *g* is more spread out, but it is still possible to calculate a mean of about 3 days, and a standard deviation of about 2 days, for both activities.

The effect of parallel activities is especially noticeable in the histogram of *g*, where the shape no longer resembles a bell curve. This is due to the fact that the duration of *g* is being measured both as the timestamp difference from *d* and the timestamp difference from *e* (or even *f*). The latter is contributing with many short measurements that accumulate towards the left side of the mean.

As for activity *a*, this is always the first task in the process, so there is no way to estimate its duration, since there is no previous event. Its duration is being shown as zero in the histogram. From the height of that column in the histogram, one can conclude that this event log had somewhere from 7000 to 8000 instances. Indeed, these data have been collected from an event log with 7549 instances.

Listing 37 Plotting the histograms of activity execution time

```
1  import numpy as np
2  import matplotlib.pyplot as plt
3
4  D = dict()
5
6  for caseid in log:
7      for i in range(0, len(log[caseid])):
8          (a, _, t) = log[caseid][i]
9          if i > 0:
10             (_, _, t0) = log[caseid][i-1]
11             d = (t-t0).total_seconds()/(24*3600)
12         else:
13             d = 0.
14         if a not in D:
15             D[a] = []
16         D[a].append(d)
17
18 nrows = 4
19 ncols = 2
20
21 fig, ax = plt.subplots(nrows, ncols)
22
23 i = 0
24 j = 0
25 for a in sorted(D.keys()):
26     print('%s: mean=%.2f std=%.2f days' % (a, np.mean(D[a]), np.std(D[a])))
27     ax[i,j].hist(D[a], bins=[0.1*k for k in range(100)])
28     ax[i,j].set_title(a)
29     ax[i,j].set_xticks(range(10))
30     ax[i,j].grid(True)
31     if i == nrows-1:
32         ax[i,j].set_xlabel('days')
33     j += 1
34     if j == ncols:
35         i += 1
36         j = 0
37
38 plt.tight_layout()
39 plt.show()
```

Listing 37 shows how Fig. 19 has been generated with Matplotlib. After reading the event log as in Listing 31 on page 49, Listing 37 goes through the event log, calculates all timestamp differences, and plots the histograms as a series of subplots.

In more detail, line 4 creates a dictionary D which will store the list of timestamp differences collected for each activity. Lines 6–7 go through each case id, and then through each event in the case id, as usual.

Line 8 retrieves the task and timestamp from the current event. If this is not the first event in the case id (line 9) then we get the timestamp from the previous event (line 10) and we calculate the timestamp difference as a number of days. If it is the first event (line 12) then the duration is set to zero (line 13).

Lines 14–15 initialize the list of timestamp differences, if the activity is not yet in dictionary D. Regardless of this initialization, the timestamp difference is appended to the list in line 16.

Lines 18–19 set the number of subplots in the figure. These subplots are arranged into rows and columns. With the specified number of rows and columns, we will have $4 \times 2 = 8$ subplots. (Alternatively, the number of rows and columns could have been set dynamically according to the number of activities in dictionary D.)

The figure is created in line 21 with a call to the `subplots()` function. This function returns a `Figure` object and an array of `Axes` objects that can be used to configure each subplot.

In lines 23–24, we initialize two variables that will be used as row and column indexes to configure each subplot in the figure.

Line 25 iterates through the activities in sorted order. In line 26, we use the NumPy library (imported in line 1) to calculate the mean and standard deviation of the activity execution time. These results are being printed as a formatted string with two decimal places for each value.

Then line 27 computes and draws the histogram of timestamp differences for each activity. In the `hist()` method, the parameter `bins` defines the bins for the histogram. Here, each bin will have a width of 0.1 days, and the bins will range from zero up to $0.1 \times 100 = 10$ days, as can be seen in Fig. 19.

Line 28 puts the activity name as the title at the top of the subplot. Line 29 sets the ticks in the x-axis, and line 30 turns on the grid. Furthermore, if we are at the last row of subplots, we give a title to the x-axis (lines 31–32).

Lines 38–39 display the plot that is shown in Fig. 19. The output of this script (as produced by line 26) is shown in Listing 38.

From this output, it is possible to confirm that the duration of activity a is not being measured, and that the longest activities are e and g. In fact, activity g has a duration that, on average, is actually higher than what is being reported in Listing 38. However, due to the effect of the parallel activities in the process, and the way the duration is being calculated, it appears to have a slightly lower mean.

Listing 38 Output of the previous script

```
1    a: mean=0.00 std=0.00 days
2    b: mean=2.13 std=1.10 days
3    c: mean=1.29 std=0.89 days
4    d: mean=1.54 std=1.49 days
5    e: mean=2.99 std=2.08 days
6    f: mean=1.74 std=1.96 days
7    g: mean=2.65 std=1.97 days
8    h: mean=2.26 std=1.21 days
```

4.9 Summary

Here is a brief summary of what we have learned in this chapter:

- The performance perspective can be analyzed on top of the control-flow perspective by calculating, for example, the average timestamp difference for each transition in control-flow graph.

- To calculate timestamp differences in Python, it is more convenient to represent the timestamps as `datetime` objects. The difference between two `datetime` objects is a `timedelta` object.
- In the performance perspective, it is often useful to plot individual events on a timeline in order to discover certain patterns and identify potential sources of delay or inefficiencies in the process.
- The timeline of individual events, which is usually called a dotted chart, can be displayed using absolute time or relative time, with the later being the time elapsed since the first event in the same case id.
- Matplotlib is a versatile plotting library for Python, which can be used to generate dotted charts and histograms, among several other kinds of plots. It is often used together with NumPy to perform numerical computations.
- The timestamp difference between consecutive events can provide only a rough estimate of the duration of each activity in the process. It is important to take into account the control-flow perspective in order to assess the results.

Chapter 5
Process Mining in Practice

Over the years, the process mining community has placed several real-world event logs in the public domain. Most of these event logs have been released in the scope of process mining competitions, where contestants could use any of the available techniques, or even develop new techniques, to discover the business process.

Once these event logs have been released, they can be used for a number of different purposes, such as testing existing tools, trying out new ideas, comparing different approaches, etc. In this chapter, we will use one of those event logs to illustrate how process mining techniques can be applied in practice.

Among the challenges of dealing with real-world data is that each event log usually has some specific characteristics. These are related either to the process which generated the event log, or to the system from which the event log was collected. Therefore, it may be necessary to use some form of preprocessing before process mining techniques can actually be applied.

In this respect, the case study presented in this chapter is no exception. To start with, the event log is stored in an XML-based format, so the first step is to parse the XML document in order to retrieve the event data. In addition, the event log contains different kinds of events, so it will be necessary to filter them in order to focus on the events of interest. While doing this, we will learn a few additional skills that turn out to be very useful in practice.

5.1 The BPI Challenge 2012

The *International Conference on Business Process Management* (BPM)[1] is the premier forum where researchers in the field of process mining (and also in the wider community of business process management) usually meet.

---

[1] http://bpm-conference.org/.

© The Author(s) 2020
D. R. Ferreira, *A Primer on Process Mining*, SpringerBriefs in Information Systems,
https://doi.org/10.1007/978-3-030-41819-9_5

Within the conference, there is usually a main track, and there are also several workshops focusing on specific topics of interest. One of these workshops is the *International Workshop on Business Process Intelligence* (BPI),[2] which has been running together with the conference since 2005. The BPI workshop focuses essentially on the development of new process mining techniques for the analysis of business processes from event data.

Since 2011, the workshop includes the *BPI Challenge*, a process mining competition where a real-world event log is made publicly available, and the community is encouraged to use any techniques, including but not limited to process mining tools, to derive meaningful business information.

In 2012, the BPI Challenge involved an event log from a Dutch financial institution.[3] The event log concerned an application process for personal loans. The process can be briefly described as follows:

> The customer submits a loan application (with a requested amount of money) through a Web page. The loan application goes through a series of checks and, if it passes, the customer is contacted by phone to provide additional information. Then, an offer is sent to the customer by mail. When the customer replies to the offer, the loan application is reassessed and, if it is incomplete, additional information is gathered by contacting the customer again. Eventually, there is a final assessment, and the loan is either approved or declined. If it is approved, the loan is also activated.

This is basically all that was known about the process. Anything else would have to be inferred from the provided event log.[4] This particular event log includes several different kinds of events, namely:

- The changes in the state of the loan application throughout the process. These events are labeled with prefix 'A_'.
- The changes in the state of the offer that is sent to the customer. These events are labeled with prefix 'O_'.
- The events associated with the scheduling, start, and completion of work items (i.e. tasks) that are performed by the employees in the organization. These events are labeled with prefix 'W_'.

Table 2 shows the first process instance recorded in the event log. Each entry in the task column has one of the prefixes 'A_', 'O_' or 'W_', as described above. Furthermore, the work items (with prefix 'W_') have a designation in Dutch. The meaning of these events is as follows:

- *W_Completeren aanvraag* – filling in the information for the loan application;
- *W_Nabellen offertes* – calling after an offer has been sent to the customer;
- *W_Valideren aanvraag* – assessing the loan application.

---

[2]https://www.win.tue.nl/bpi/.

[3]http://www.win.tue.nl/bpi/doku.php?id=2012:challenge.

[4]http://dx.doi.org/10.4121/uuid:3926db30-f712-4394-aebc-75976070e91f.

Table 2 Event log of the BPI Challenge 2012 (excerpt)

Case id	Task	Event type	User	Timestamp
173688	A_SUBMITTED	COMPLETE	112	2011-10-01 00:38:44
173688	A_PARTLYSUBMITTED	COMPLETE	112	2011-10-01 00:38:44
173688	A_PREACCEPTED	COMPLETE	112	2011-10-01 00:39:37
173688	W_Completeren aanvraag	SCHEDULE	112	2011-10-01 00:39:38
173688	W_Completeren aanvraag	START	–	2011-10-01 11:36:46
173688	A_ACCEPTED	COMPLETE	10862	2011-10-01 11:42:43
173688	O_SELECTED	COMPLETE	10862	2011-10-01 11:45:09
173688	A_FINALIZED	COMPLETE	10862	2011-10-01 11:45:09
173688	O_CREATED	COMPLETE	10862	2011-10-01 11:45:11
173688	O_SENT	COMPLETE	10862	2011-10-01 11:45:11
173688	W_Nabellen offertes	SCHEDULE	–	2011-10-01 11:45:11
173688	W_Completeren aanvraag	COMPLETE	–	2011-10-01 11:45:13
173688	W_Nabellen offertes	START	–	2011-10-01 12:15:41
173688	W_Nabellen offertes	COMPLETE	–	2011-10-01 12:17:08
173688	W_Nabellen offertes	START	10913	2011-10-08 16:26:57
173688	W_Nabellen offertes	COMPLETE	10913	2011-10-08 16:32:00
173688	W_Nabellen offertes	START	11049	2011-10-10 11:32:22
173688	O_SENT_BACK	COMPLETE	11049	2011-10-10 11:33:03
173688	W_Valideren aanvraag	SCHEDULE	11049	2011-10-10 11:33:04
173688	W_Nabellen offertes	COMPLETE	11049	2011-10-10 11:33:05
173688	W_Valideren aanvraag	START	10629	2011-10-13 10:05:26
173688	A_REGISTERED	COMPLETE	10629	2011-10-13 10:37:29
173688	A_APPROVED	COMPLETE	10629	2011-10-13 10:37:29
173688	O_ACCEPTED	COMPLETE	10629	2011-10-13 10:37:29
173688	A_ACTIVATED	COMPLETE	10629	2011-10-13 10:37:29
173688	W_Valideren aanvraag	COMPLETE	10629	2011-10-13 10:37:37

Besides the case id, task, user, and timestamp columns, Table 2 includes an additional column that we designate here by *event type*. For the tasks with prefix 'A_' and 'O_' (states of the application and states of the offer, respectively) the event type is always COMPLETE and it might as well have been omitted. It is for the tasks with prefix 'W_' (work items) that the event type is meaningful.

The SCHEDULE event type means that the work item has been enqueued for execution (much like the assignment of tasks to users as depicted in Fig. 2 on page 4). The START event type means that someone has started working on the task, and the COMPLETE event type means that the task has been completed.

Usually, in practice, only events of type COMPLETE are available. However, in this particular event log, the scheduling, start and completion of each task have also been recorded. We will make use of this information when analyzing the performance perspective. For the control-flow perspective and for the organizational perspective, we will focus mainly on COMPLETE events.

5.2   Understanding the XES Format

The event log for the BPI Challenge 2012 is provided in two alternative formats: XES (Extensible Event Stream) [23] and MXML (Mining XML) [21]. Both are XML-based formats for storing and exchanging event logs. XES is the newer format that has been approved as a standard by IEEE.[5] MXML (Mining XML) [21] is the older format that has been long supported by the ProM framework [22].

While XES is expected to completely replace MXML, there are still some event logs in MXML format, particularly from the times that predate XES. It is possible to convert an event log in MXML to the newer format by importing it in ProM[6] and then exporting it to XES. Another option is to use the OpenXES[7] library, which is a reference implementation of the XES standard in Java.

Here we will be working with the event log in XES format, which is also the original format in which the data have been published for the BPI Challenge 2012. In fact, the MXML version of the event log was produced by backward conversion from XES to MXML using the OpenXES library. This has been done for the convenience of users who, at the time of the BPI Challenge 2012, were using process mining tools that did not yet support XES.

Listing 39 shows the first few events of the event log in XES format.

This is an XML document where the root element is `<log>`. It contains a series of traces (i.e. cases or process instances), with each trace being delimited by the opening tag `<trace>` and the closing tag `</trace>`. Listing 39 shows a single trace, but in general there will be multiple traces, one for each process instance. Each trace has a list of events, and each event is enclosed by an `<event>` element.

Both `<trace>` and `<event>` elements may have several children, in the form of `<string>` or `<date>` elements. Of special interest is the `<string>` element with the attribute `key="concept:name"`. In a trace, such element provides the case id. For example, in Listing 39 the case id of the trace being presented is 173688 (line 6). This is the same process instance that has been listed earlier in Table 2.

In an event, the `<string>` element with the attribute `key="concept:name"` provides the task name. For example, in Listing 39 the three events being presented correspond to the tasks A_SUBMITTED, A_PARTLYSUBMITTED, and A_PREACCEPTED (lines 11, 17 and 23, respectively).

The other child elements in an event also contain important information regarding the task. The `<string>` element with the attribute `key="org:resource"` contains the user who is associated with the task, and the `<date>` element with the attribute `key="time:timestamp"` contains the timestamp of the event.

The `<string>` element with the attribute `key="lifecycle:transition"` is a standard XES extension that can be used to denote the event type. When a task goes

---

[5]http://www.xes-standard.org/.

[6]http://www.promtools.org/.

[7]http://www.xes-standard.org/openxes/.

Listing 39 Event log in XES format (excerpt)

```
1   <?xml version="1.0" encoding="UTF-8"?>
2   <log xes.version="1.0" ... xmlns="http://www.xes-standard.org/">
3      ...
4      <trace>
5         <date key="REG_DATE" value="2011-10-01T00:38:44.546+02:00"/>
6         <string key="concept:name" value="173688"/>
7         <string key="AMOUNT_REQ" value="20000"/>
8         <event>
9            <string key="org:resource" value="112"/>
10           <string key="lifecycle:transition" value="COMPLETE"/>
11           <string key="concept:name" value="A_SUBMITTED"/>
12           <date key="time:timestamp" value="2011-10-01T00:38:44.546+02:00"/>
13        </event>
14        <event>
15           <string key="org:resource" value="112"/>
16           <string key="lifecycle:transition" value="COMPLETE"/>
17           <string key="concept:name" value="A_PARTLYSUBMITTED"/>
18           <date key="time:timestamp" value="2011-10-01T00:38:44.880+02:00"/>
19        </event>
20        <event>
21           <string key="org:resource" value="112"/>
22           <string key="lifecycle:transition" value="COMPLETE"/>
23           <string key="concept:name" value="A_PREACCEPTED"/>
24           <date key="time:timestamp" value="2011-10-01T00:39:37.906+02:00"/>
25        </event>
26        ...
27     </trace>
28     ...
29  </log>
```

through multiple states (such as SCHEDULE, START and COMPLETE in this event log), then this extension is used to denote such state. Listing 40 shows an example.

Here, the same task (*W_Completeren aanvraag*) has resulted in three different events being recorded in the trace. The first event was recorded when the task was scheduled (SCHEDULE in line 11), a second event when the task was started (START in line 17) and a third event when the task was completed (COMPLETE in line 23).

As described in the previous section, this only happens for the tasks with prefix 'W_' (work items). In addition, for the analysis of the control-flow and organizational perspectives, it usually suffices to consider only COMPLETE events. However, the interested reader may refer to [10, 26] for other approaches that take into account both START and COMPLETE event types.

Finally, both in Listing 39 and in Listing 40 one can observe that there are some additional child elements within a <trace> that are outside events (lines 5–7). Besides the <string> element with key="concept:name" that provides the case id, the <string> element with key="AMOUNT_REQ" contains the amount of money requested for the loan, and the <date> element with key="REG_DATE" contains the date and time when the loan application was first registered.

These extra elements will not be used in our analysis, but it is worth noting that possibility of having these extensions to traces and events was one of the main reasons for the development of XES. Whereas MXML was a rather strict and restricted format, XES offers the possibility of including custom data in an event

Listing 40 Use of the lifecycle extension in XES

```
 1    <?xml version="1.0" encoding="UTF-8"?>
 2    <log xes.version="1.0" ... xmlns="http://www.xes-standard.org/">
 3        ...
 4        <trace>
 5            <date key="REG_DATE" value="2011-10-01T00:38:44.546+02:00"/>
 6            <string key="concept:name" value="173688"/>
 7            <string key="AMOUNT_REQ" value="20000"/>
 8            ...
 9            <event>
10                <string key="org:resource" value="112"/>
11                <string key="lifecycle:transition" value="SCHEDULE"/>
12                <string key="concept:name" value="W_Completeren aanvraag"/>
13                <date key="time:timestamp" value="2011-10-01T00:39:38.875+02:00"/>
14            </event>
15            <event>
16                <string key="concept:name" value="W_Completeren aanvraag"/>
17                <string key="lifecycle:transition" value="START"/>
18                <date key="time:timestamp" value="2011-10-01T11:36:46.437+02:00"/>
19            </event>
20            ...
21            <event>
22                <string key="concept:name" value="W_Completeren aanvraag"/>
23                <string key="lifecycle:transition" value="COMPLETE"/>
24                <date key="time:timestamp" value="2011-10-01T11:45:13.917+02:00"/>
25            </event>
26            ...
27        </trace>
28        ...
29    </log>
```

log. These custom data can be used for other kinds of analysis such as, for example, classifying loan applications according to the requested amount.

5.3   Reading XES with Python

Reading a XES event log with Python is essentially an exercise in XML parsing. The Python standard library already includes an XML parser known as ElementTree.[8] Since this parser is readily available in every Python distribution, it is the simplest option to use for our purposes.

Listing 41 shows how to parse the XES event log with ElementTree. The first thing to do is to load the XML document into an element tree, and then get the root element of that tree (lines 4–5). From the root element, it is possible to search for specific elements in the tree.

If the XML document contains namespaces, it will be necessary to prepend each element with its corresponding namespace. In general, XES event logs make use of the namespace http://www.xes-standard.org/, as shown both in Listing 39 and in Listing 40 (line 2).

---

[8]https://docs.python.org/3/library/xml.etree.elementtree.html.

Listing 41 Parsing a XES event log with ElementTree

```
1   import datetime
2   import xml.etree.ElementTree as ET
3
4   tree = ET.parse('financial_log.xes')
5   root = tree.getroot()
6
7   ns = {'xes': 'http://www.xes-standard.org/'}
8
9   for trace in root.findall('xes:trace', ns):
10      caseid = ''
11      for string in trace.findall('xes:string', ns):
12          if string.attrib['key'] == 'concept:name':
13              caseid = string.attrib['value']
14      for event in trace.findall('xes:event', ns):
15          task = ''
16          user = ''
17          event_type = ''
18          for string in event.findall('xes:string', ns):
19              if string.attrib['key'] == 'concept:name':
20                  task = string.attrib['value']
21              if string.attrib['key'] == 'org:resource':
22                  user = string.attrib['value']
23              if string.attrib['key'] == 'lifecycle:transition':
24                  event_type = string.attrib['value']
25          timestamp = ''
26          for date in event.findall('xes:date', ns):
27              if date.attrib['key'] == 'time:timestamp':
28                  timestamp = date.attrib['value']
29                  timestamp = datetime.datetime.strptime(timestamp[:-10],
30                                              '%Y-%m-%dT%H:%M:%S')
31          print(';'.join([caseid, task, event_type, user, str(timestamp)]))
```

Therefore, when searching for elements in the XML tree, we must provide this namespace, and this is the reason why such namespace is being defined in Listing 41 (line 7). The namespaces are defined in a dictionary where each key is a prefix that stands for a given namespace. In Listing 40 there is only one namespace, but there could be more, if several namespaces were being used.

The first search for elements occurs in line 9, where we iterate through all <trace> elements in the event log. The element name must be prepended with the prefix 'xes:' to specify that it is within the XES namespace.

For each trace, the case id is in a <string> element with a key attribute with the value concept:name. Line 11 finds all <string> elements in a trace, and line 12 checks the key attribute in each of them. (As shown in line 12, the list of attributes can be accessed as a dictionary.) When the desired <string> element is found, the case id can be obtained from its value attribute (line 13).

A very similar approach is being used to iterate through all events in a trace (line 14) and retrieve the task, user, and event type (lines 18–24). As for the timestamp, this can be found in a date element instead (lines 26–28).

In lines 29–30, the timestamp is converted into to a datetime object. For simplicity, the milliseconds and the time zone information are discarded by ignoring the last 10 characters in the timestamp. However, if desired, it would be possible to parse the milliseconds with the %f directive and, with some extra work, the time zone too (with the %z directive, if available).

Listing 42 Output of the previous script (excerpt)

```
1   173688;A_SUBMITTED;COMPLETE;112;2011-10-01 00:38:44
2   173688;A_PARTLYSUBMITTED;COMPLETE;112;2011-10-01 00:38:44
3   173688;A_PREACCEPTED;COMPLETE;112;2011-10-01 00:39:37
4   173688;W_Completeren aanvraag;SCHEDULE;112;2011-10-01 00:39:38
5   173688;W_Completeren aanvraag;START;;2011-10-01 11:36:46
6   173688;A_ACCEPTED;COMPLETE;10862;2011-10-01 11:42:43
7   173688;O_SELECTED;COMPLETE;10862;2011-10-01 11:45:09
8   173688;A_FINALIZED;COMPLETE;10862;2011-10-01 11:45:09
9   173688;O_CREATED;COMPLETE;10862;2011-10-01 11:45:11
10  173688;O_SENT;COMPLETE;10862;2011-10-01 11:45:11
11  173688;W_Nabellen offertes;SCHEDULE;;2011-10-01 11:45:11
12  173688;W_Completeren aanvraag;COMPLETE;;2011-10-01 11:45:13
13  173688;W_Nabellen offertes;START;;2011-10-01 12:15:41
14  173688;W_Nabellen offertes;COMPLETE;;2011-10-01 12:17:08
15  173688;W_Nabellen offertes;START;10913;2011-10-08 16:26:57
16  173688;W_Nabellen offertes;COMPLETE;10913;2011-10-08 16:32:00
17  173688;W_Nabellen offertes;START;11049;2011-10-10 11:32:22
18  173688;O_SENT_BACK;COMPLETE;11049;2011-10-10 11:33:03
19  173688;W_Valideren aanvraag;SCHEDULE;11049;2011-10-10 11:33:04
20  173688;W_Nabellen offertes;COMPLETE;11049;2011-10-10 11:33:05
21  173688;W_Valideren aanvraag;START;10629;2011-10-13 10:05:26
22  173688;A_REGISTERED;COMPLETE;10629;2011-10-13 10:37:29
23  173688;A_APPROVED;COMPLETE;10629;2011-10-13 10:37:29
24  173688;O_ACCEPTED;COMPLETE;10629;2011-10-13 10:37:29
25  173688;A_ACTIVATED;COMPLETE;10629;2011-10-13 10:37:29
26  173688;W_Valideren aanvraag;COMPLETE;10629;2011-10-13 10:37:37
```

Finally, in line 31, the script joins all the fields into a single line, using the semicolon as separator. The end result is shown in Listing 42. This output can be redirected to a file, in order to store the event log in CSV format.

5.4 Analyzing the Control-Flow Perspective

With the script in Listing 41, the event log from the BPI Challenge 2012 has been converted from XES to CSV. We can now apply to this event log the same code and techniques developed in the previous chapters.

For example, it is possible to use the code in Listing 19 on page 29 to analyze the event log from the control-flow perspective. However, this particular event log can be seen as comprising three different sub-processes:

- the changes in the state of the loan application, i.e. the events with prefix 'A_';
- the changes in the state of the offer that is sent to the customer, with prefix 'O_';
- the changes in the state of work items, i.e. the events with prefix 'W_';

For this particular event log, it is more convenient to conduct a separate analysis of these different kinds of events, which provides a more compact and understandable view of the behavior in the business process.

Figure 20 shows the control-flow graph for the events with prefix 'A_'. From this graph, it becomes apparent that the loan application starts in a submitted state, and ends with one of three outcomes: declined, canceled, or approved.

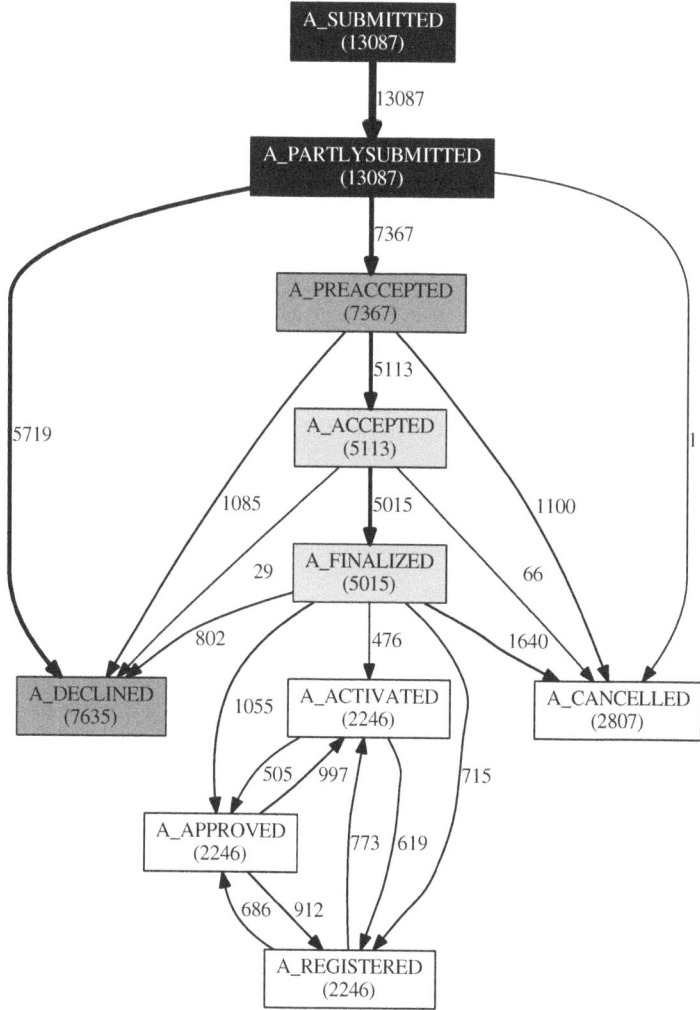

Fig. 20 Control-flow graph for the states of the loan application

In fact, the loan application can be declined or canceled at different stages in the process. Of those applications that end up being declined, most are declined at an early stage, when some preliminary checks are being performed. In contrast, only one application was ever canceled at such an early stage; most applications end up being canceled at later states in the process.

When the loan application is approved, it must also be registered and activated. From the reciprocal edges between these states in Fig. 20, one can suspect that these three events can happen in any order. Indeed, an inspection of Listing 42 shows that

Fig. 21 Control-flow graph
for the states of the offer

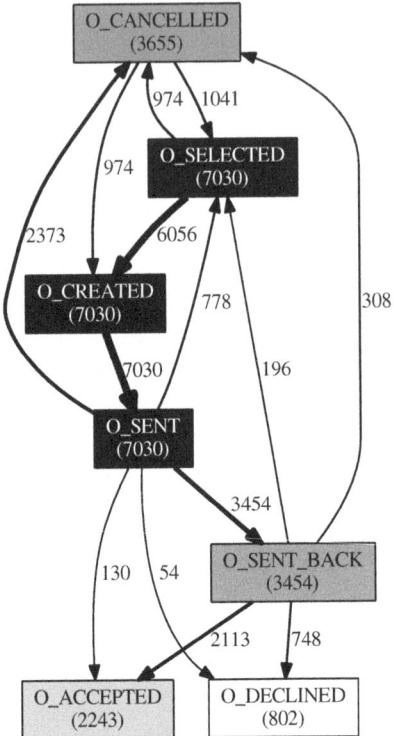

these three events have been recorded at the same time, so their order is probably interchangeable.

The analysis of the events with prefix 'o_' (offers) is shown in Fig. 21. Here it is not immediately clear in which state the offer begins, because Graphviz has placed the canceled state at the top. Anyway, the color shading of nodes and their activity counts point us to the conclusion that the offer starts in the selected state, goes to the created stated, and then to the sent state.

After the offer has been sent to the customer, it may end up being canceled if the customer does not reply. If the customer sends back the offer, it can still be canceled, but only a minority of cases end up going that way. The most common scenario is for the sent back offer to be either accepted or declined.

From the graph in Fig. 21, it appears that even a canceled offer can sometimes be recovered and re-enter the negotiation phase with the customer.

Moving on to the events with prefix 'w_' (work items), Fig. 22 shows the sequence of tasks, where only COMPLETE events have been considered. Even so, there are still a number of transitions between the same task (i.e. self-loops in the graph). This suggests that those tasks are being performed in several steps rather than all-at-once.

Again, it is not immediately obvious where the flow begins, but the node shading and activity counts are helpful in this respect. Most instances start in a stage where

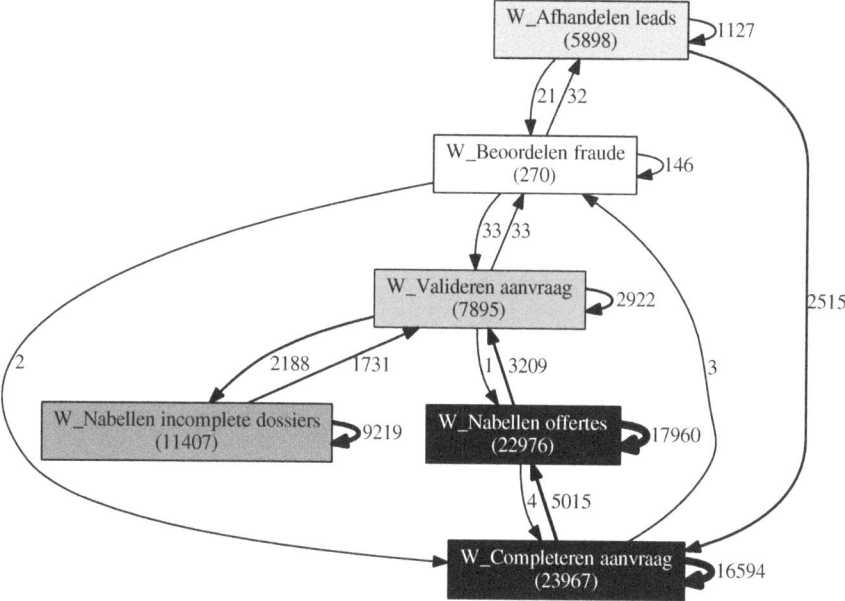

Fig. 22 Control-flow graph for the completion of work items

the information for the loan application is being filled in and an offer is being prepared for the customer (*W_Completeren aanvraag*). Some loan applications may come as a result of a previous business lead (*W_Afhandelen leads*). A few applications are also checked for possible fraud (*W_Beoordelen fraude*).

The next stage is to contact the customer about the offer (*W_Nabellen offertes*) and then, if there is a follow-up, the application is assessed (*W_Valideren aanvraag*). During assessment it may be necessary to contact the customer again to gather some missing information (*W_Nabellen incomplete dossiers*).

5.5 Analyzing the Organizational Perspective

In the organizational perspective, our analysis of the BPI Challenge 2012 event log will be focusing mainly on working together, since an analysis of handover of work leads to essentially the same conclusions.

As in the control-flow perspective, we will analyze each subprocess separately by looking at the events with a certain prefix (i.e. 'A_', 'O_' or 'W_'). An analysis of the events with prefix 'A_' yields a graph similar to the one in Fig. 23.

From this graph, it appears that everyone works together with user 112. In fact, there are reasons to believe that user 112 represents an automated system rather than a human resource. The reasons are the following:

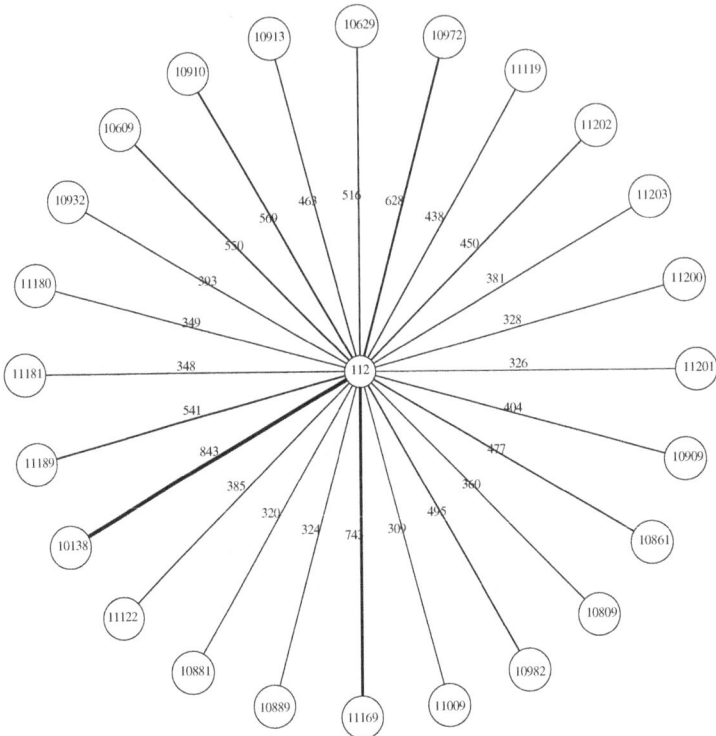

Fig. 23 Working together graph of application states, with a minimum edge count of 300

- user 112 is associated with many events that are either simultaneous or happen very close in time (see Table 2 on page 67);
- user 112 is associated with the first few events of every process instance, which correspond to the submission of a loan application by a customer, and to the automatic checks that are performed on that application;
- user 112 does not appear associated with changes in the state of an offer, nor with the completion of any work item (although it does appear associated with the scheduling of some work items).

These facts lead to the conclusion that user 112 is a system account that performs some automated tasks related to the state of the loan application in an initial stage of the process. This initial stage ends with the loan application being either pre-accepted or automatically declined. If the application is pre-accepted, then user 112 also schedules the first task to be performed by an employee.

To generate the graph in Fig. 23, it is important to note that the graph is being drawn only with those nodes and edges for which the edge count (i.e. the number of shared cases) is at least 300. In other words, an edge is added to the graph only if the corresponding value in the working together matrix is above that threshold.

This is an effective way of simplifying what would otherwise be an unnecessarily complex graph. Without such threshold, many other interactions between users would appear, but they would not be as strong as their connections to user 112, which is the main feature that Fig. 23 intends to illustrate.

Another important detail is that the graph is being generated with the `circo` program rather than `dot`. The `circo` program is a Graphviz utility that creates graphs with circular layouts. That is why the graph in Fig. 23 has a circular appearance. This is often a more convenient layout for the kind of graphs that are generated in the organizational perspective.

As a rule of thumb, `dot` is usually better for models where there is some kind of sequence flow, as in the control-flow perspective. When models become similar to networks, with a lot of interactions between a large number of nodes, then `circo` may provide a more readable graph layout.

Another graph with a circular layout is shown in Fig. 24. This is the working together graph that is obtained when considering the events with prefix 'w_'.

The graph is densely connected, and it will become even more so if we lower the threshold on the edge count, which was kept at 300. This suggests that, apparently, there are no structured teams to handle a loan application. Each employee can

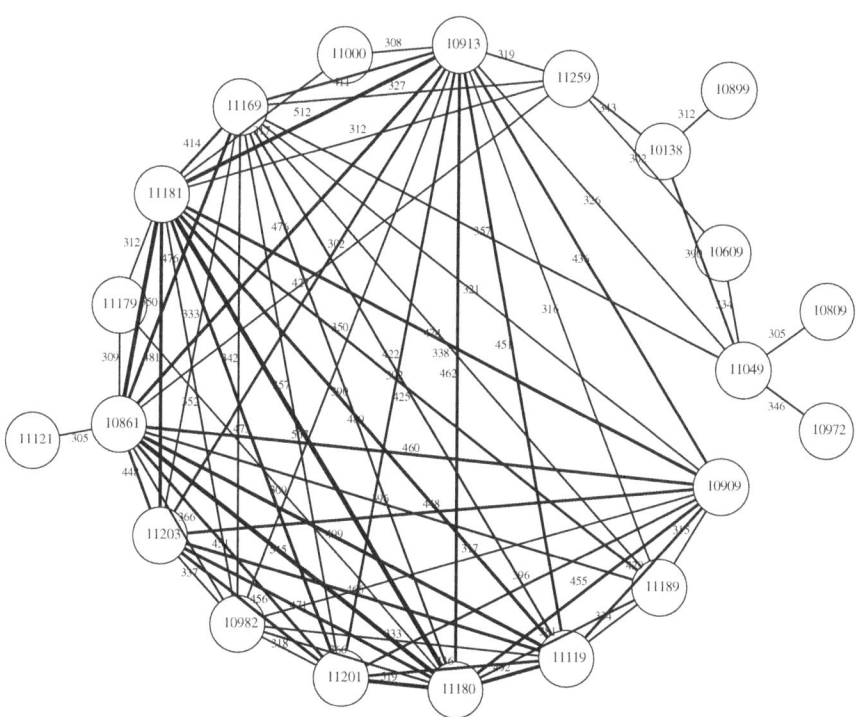

Fig. 24 Working together graph of work items, with a minimum edge count of 300

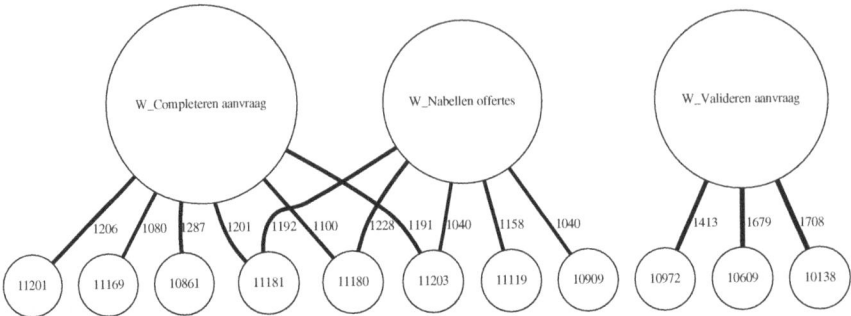

Fig. 25 Distribution of work items across users, with a minimum edge count of 1000

work with many other employees, and their collaboration seems to be mainly circumstantial, probably based on availability.

Nevertheless, it is still possible to identify groups of users who appear to have different roles. If we analyze the distribution of work items across users, then we can obtain the graph shown in Fig. 25.

From this graph, we can see that there is a group of users who complete the loan application (*W_Completeren aanvraag*) and another group of users who take care of contacting the customer about an offer (*W_Nabellen offertes*), and that there is some overlap between these two groups.

On the other hand, the group of users who are responsible for assessing the loan application (*W_Valideren aanvraag*) seems to be completely separate, at least with the relatively high threshold that has been used to generate this graph.

Since there are multiple possible users for each activity, it is not surprising to find that, at run-time, any of those users may be called in to perform the task. This may explain why it is hard to identify any concrete collaboration teams.

To generate the graphs in Figs. 24 and 25, it is important to check if the user is a non-empty string. As illustrated in Table 2 on page 67, some events have no associated user. This could create some problems if we were analyzing the handover of work. However, for working together this is not much of a problem, since we are analyzing the set (not the sequence) of users who participate in each case id.

5.6 Analyzing the Performance Perspective

In this event log, the tasks (with prefix 'w_') that are carried out by employees are recorded with SCHEDULE, START and COMPLETE events. This makes it possible to perform several different time measurements related to those tasks.

For example, by calculating the timestamp difference between the START and COMPLETE events for a given work item, we can determine exactly how much time was spent on that work item.

Consider, for example, the task *W_Completeren aanvraag* that is highlighted in Table 3. The START and COMPLETE events for this task are separated by a series of changes in the state of the loan application, and in the state of the offer that is sent to the customer (the 'A_' and 'O_' events, respectively).

Table 3 Measuring the time between START and COMPLETE events

Case id	Task	Event type	User	Timestamp
173688	A_SUBMITTED	COMPLETE	112	2011-10-01 00:38:44
173688	A_PARTLYSUBMITTED	COMPLETE	112	2011-10-01 00:38:44
173688	A_PREACCEPTED	COMPLETE	112	2011-10-01 00:39:37
173688	W_Completeren aanvraag	SCHEDULE	112	2011-10-01 00:39:38
173688	W_Completeren aanvraag	START	–	2011-10-01 11:36:46
173688	A_ACCEPTED	COMPLETE	10862	2011-10-01 11:42:43
173688	O_SELECTED	COMPLETE	10862	2011-10-01 11:45:09
173688	A_FINALIZED	COMPLETE	10862	2011-10-01 11:45:09
173688	O_CREATED	COMPLETE	10862	2011-10-01 11:45:11
173688	O_SENT	COMPLETE	10862	2011-10-01 11:45:11
173688	W_Nabellen offertes	SCHEDULE	–	2011-10-01 11:45:11
173688	W_Completeren aanvraag	COMPLETE	–	2011-10-01 11:45:13
173688	W_Nabellen offertes	START	–	2011-10-01 12:15:41
173688	W_Nabellen offertes	COMPLETE	–	2011-10-01 12:17:08
173688	W_Nabellen offertes	START	10913	2011-10-08 16:26:57
173688	W_Nabellen offertes	COMPLETE	10913	2011-10-08 16:32:00
173688	W_Nabellen offertes	START	11049	2011-10-10 11:32:22
173688	O_SENT_BACK	COMPLETE	11049	2011-10-10 11:33:03
173688	W_Valideren aanvraag	SCHEDULE	11049	2011-10-10 11:33:04
173688	W_Nabellen offertes	COMPLETE	11049	2011-10-10 11:33:05
173688	W_Valideren aanvraag	START	10629	2011-10-13 10:05:26
173688	A_REGISTERED	COMPLETE	10629	2011-10-13 10:37:29
173688	A_APPROVED	COMPLETE	10629	2011-10-13 10:37:29
173688	O_ACCEPTED	COMPLETE	10629	2011-10-13 10:37:29
173688	A_ACTIVATED	COMPLETE	10629	2011-10-13 10:37:29
173688	W_Valideren aanvraag	COMPLETE	10629	2011-10-13 10:37:37

Looking at the timestamps of these events, it is very likely that these changes in state are being produced while the task (*W_Completeren aanvraag*) is being performed. Eventually, *W_Completeren aanvraag* finishes, but not before scheduling the next task (*W_Nabellen offertes*).

By taking the timestamp difference between the START and COMPLETE events for *W_Completeren aanvraag*, we can determine exactly how much time was spent on this task. If we carry out the same analysis throughout the entire event log, we find that, on average, each work item takes somewhere between 10 and 20 min to complete, with *W_Valideren aanvraag* being the longest.

However, Table 3 also shows that there may be several START and COMPLETE events for the same work item. Consider, for example, *W_Nabellen offertes*. After this task has been scheduled, it appears that multiple people have been working on it at different points in time.

Therefore, to calculate the effective working time that was spent on each work item, we could sum all the timestamp differences between the START and COMPLETE events for that work item. If we carry out this analysis, we find that, on average, the effective time spent on each work item is somewhere between 20 and 60 min, with *W_Nabellen incomplete dossiers* being the longest one.

Another analysis that can be conducted is to measure the entire life span of a work item by considering the timestamp difference between the first START event and the last COMPLETE event, or even the timestamp difference between the initial SCHEDULE event and the final COMPLETE event for that work item.

Table 4 illustrates the measurement between the initial SCHEDULE event and the final COMPLETE event for each work item. If we carry out this analysis for the whole event log, we find that the average life span of each work item is somewhere between 2 and 12 days, with *W_Nabellen offertes* being the longest one.

On the other hand, Table 5 illustrates the measurement of the waiting time between the initial SCHEDULE event and the first START event for each work item. If we carry out this analysis for the whole event log, we find that the average waiting time for each work item is somewhere between 1 and 3 days, with *W_Nabellen offertes* being the longest one again.

From these results, we conclude that the waiting time may account for some, but not all of the entire life span of each work item. This life span can be quite long (several days) despite the fact that the effective working time is relatively short (up to 1 h). This happens because each activity is being carried out in several short steps over a relatively long period of time.

Table 4 Measuring the time between SCHEDULE and COMPLETE events

Case id	Task	Event type	User	Timestamp
173688	A_SUBMITTED	COMPLETE	112	2011-10-01 00:38:44
173688	A_PARTLYSUBMITTED	COMPLETE	112	2011-10-01 00:38:44
173688	A_PREACCEPTED	COMPLETE	112	2011-10-01 00:39:37
173688	W_Completeren aanvraag	SCHEDULE	112	2011-10-01 00:39:38
173688	W_Completeren aanvraag	START	–	2011-10-01 11:36:46
173688	A_ACCEPTED	COMPLETE	10862	2011-10-01 11:42:43
173688	O_SELECTED	COMPLETE	10862	2011-10-01 11:45:09
173688	A_FINALIZED	COMPLETE	10862	2011-10-01 11:45:09
173688	O_CREATED	COMPLETE	10862	2011-10-01 11:45:11
173688	O_SENT	COMPLETE	10862	2011-10-01 11:45:11
173688	W_Nabellen offertes	SCHEDULE	–	2011-10-01 11:45:11
173688	W_Completeren aanvraag	COMPLETE	–	2011-10-01 11:45:13
173688	W_Nabellen offertes	START	–	2011-10-01 12:15:41
173688	W_Nabellen offertes	COMPLETE	–	2011-10-01 12:17:08
173688	W_Nabellen offertes	START	10913	2011-10-08 16:26:57
173688	W_Nabellen offertes	COMPLETE	10913	2011-10-08 16:32:00
173688	W_Nabellen offertes	START	11049	2011-10-10 11:32:22
173688	O_SENT_BACK	COMPLETE	11049	2011-10-10 11:33:03
173688	W_Valideren aanvraag	SCHEDULE	11049	2011-10-10 11:33:04
173688	W_Nabellen offertes	COMPLETE	11049	2011-10-10 11:33:05
173688	W_Valideren aanvraag	START	10629	2011-10-13 10:05:26
173688	A_REGISTERED	COMPLETE	10629	2011-10-13 10:37:29
173688	A_APPROVED	COMPLETE	10629	2011-10-13 10:37:29
173688	O_ACCEPTED	COMPLETE	10629	2011-10-13 10:37:29
173688	A_ACTIVATED	COMPLETE	10629	2011-10-13 10:37:29
173688	W_Valideren aanvraag	COMPLETE	10629	2011-10-13 10:37:37

The most dramatic example is *W_Nabellen offertes* with, on average, 35 min of working time for a total life span of 12 days. However, this is not too worrisome because it concerns the negotiation of an offer through several contacts with a customer over a possibly long period of time. The performance of this activity depends on factors that are beyond the internal resources of the organization.

A more interesting example is *W_Valideren aanvraag* with 33 min of working time for a total life span of 2.1 days, of which 1.8 days are spent on just waiting for someone to pick up the task. This waiting time seems to be due to the fact that there are relatively few employees with the responsibility of assessing loan applications, as we have seen in the analysis of the organizational perspective. It could be that these resources are somewhat overloaded.

Table 5 Measuring the time between SCHEDULE and START events

Case id	Task	Event type	User	Timestamp
173688	A_SUBMITTED	COMPLETE	112	2011-10-01 00:38:44
173688	A_PARTLYSUBMITTED	COMPLETE	112	2011-10-01 00:38:44
173688	A_PREACCEPTED	COMPLETE	112	2011-10-01 00:39:37
173688	W_Completeren aanvraag	SCHEDULE	112	2011-10-01 00:39:38
173688	W_Completeren aanvraag	START	–	2011-10-01 11:36:46
173688	A_ACCEPTED	COMPLETE	10862	2011-10-01 11:42:43
173688	O_SELECTED	COMPLETE	10862	2011-10-01 11:45:09
173688	A_FINALIZED	COMPLETE	10862	2011-10-01 11:45:09
173688	O_CREATED	COMPLETE	10862	2011-10-01 11:45:11
173688	O_SENT	COMPLETE	10862	2011-10-01 11:45:11
173688	W_Nabellen offertes	SCHEDULE	–	2011-10-01 11:45:11
173688	W_Completeren aanvraag	COMPLETE	–	2011-10-01 11:45:13
173688	W_Nabellen offertes	START	–	2011-10-01 12:15:41
173688	W_Nabellen offertes	COMPLETE	–	2011-10-01 12:17:08
173688	W_Nabellen offertes	START	10913	2011-10-08 16:26:57
173688	W_Nabellen offertes	COMPLETE	10913	2011-10-08 16:32:00
173688	W_Nabellen offertes	START	11049	2011-10-10 11:32:22
173688	O_SENT_BACK	COMPLETE	11049	2011-10-10 11:33:03
173688	W_Valideren aanvraag	SCHEDULE	11049	2011-10-10 11:33:04
173688	W_Nabellen offertes	COMPLETE	11049	2011-10-10 11:33:05
173688	W_Valideren aanvraag	START	10629	2011-10-13 10:05:26
173688	A_REGISTERED	COMPLETE	10629	2011-10-13 10:37:29
173688	A_APPROVED	COMPLETE	10629	2011-10-13 10:37:29
173688	O_ACCEPTED	COMPLETE	10629	2011-10-13 10:37:29
173688	A_ACTIVATED	COMPLETE	10629	2011-10-13 10:37:29
173688	W_Valideren aanvraag	COMPLETE	10629	2011-10-13 10:37:37

5.7 Process Mining with Disco

Disco[9] is a process mining tool created by Fluxicon, a start-up company founded by
two PhD graduates from the Eindhoven University of Technology. Disco is quite a
user-friendly tool, where one will find his or her way around quite easily, at least for
someone who is already familiar with process mining.

The starting point for using the tool is to open a log file, which can be either in
CSV or in XES format. If the log file is a CSV, it will be necessary to choose which
columns will be used as case id, task, user, and timestamp. In Disco, the task and
user columns are referred to as *activity* and *resource*, respectively.

---

[9]https://fluxicon.com/disco/.

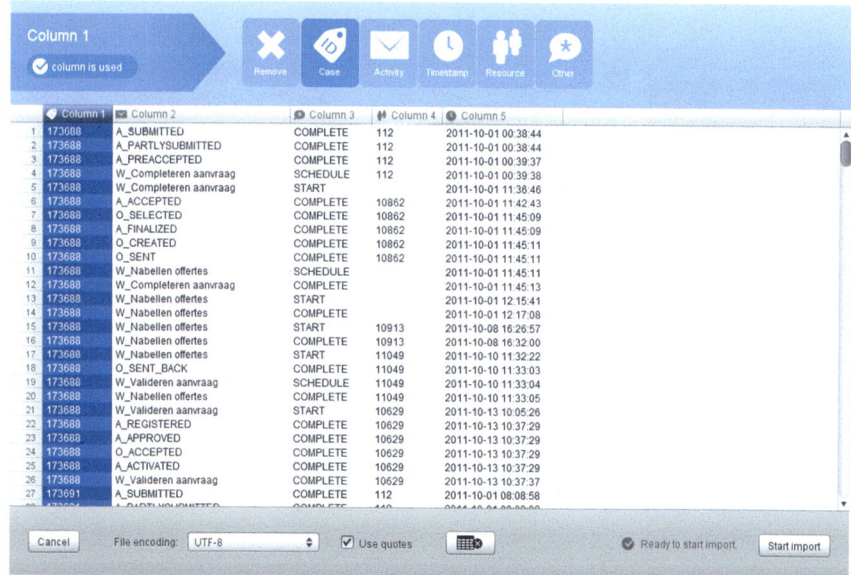

Fig. 26 Opening a log file in Disco

Figure 26 shows the screen where the user can click on a column and select one of the icons on top in order to indicate the purpose of that column. In Fig. 26, column 1 is highlighted, and the selected icon (*case*) means that this column will be used as case id. The remaining columns can be configured in a similar way: column 2 as *activity*, column 4 as *resource*, and column 5 as *timestamp*.

Column 3 is the event type, but there is no predefined role for it in Disco. However, if we would like to filter events based on event type, then we should definitely keep this column, by marking it as *Other*. Any column that is left unmarked at this stage will be unavailable in subsequent stages.

By marking column 3 as *Other*, it is possible to define a filter based on the values that appear in this column. In Fig. 27, we have defined a filter to select the events of type COMPLETE and ignore the START and SCHEDULE events.

A similar filter can be used to select the events with a certain task prefix ('A_', 'O_' or 'W_'). In Fig. 28, we have defined a second filter to keep the tasks with prefix 'W_' and ignore the tasks with prefixes 'A_' and 'O_'.

After applying both filters to the event log, Disco generates the control-flow graph shown in Fig. 29. In Disco, this graph is called a *process map*, and it has an implicit start node to denote where the control flow begins, and an implicit end node to denote where the control flow ends.

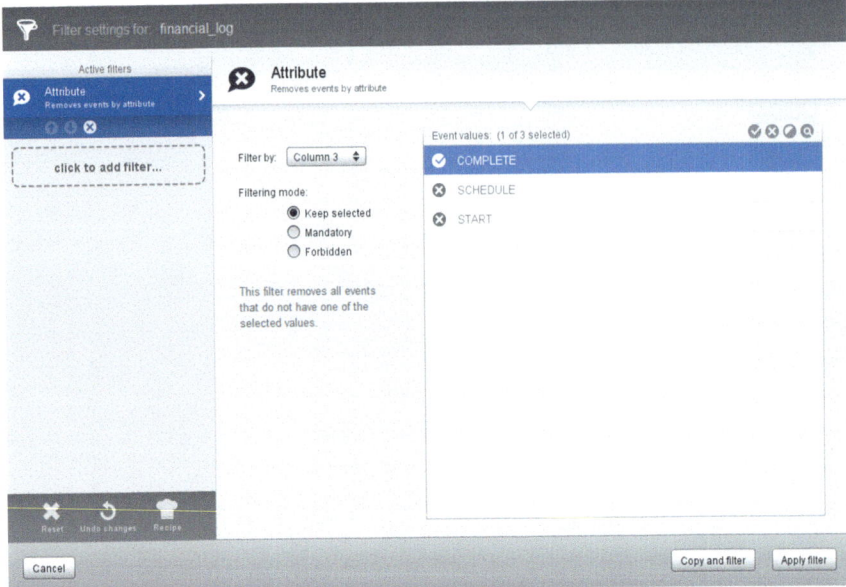

Fig. 27 Applying a filter on event type

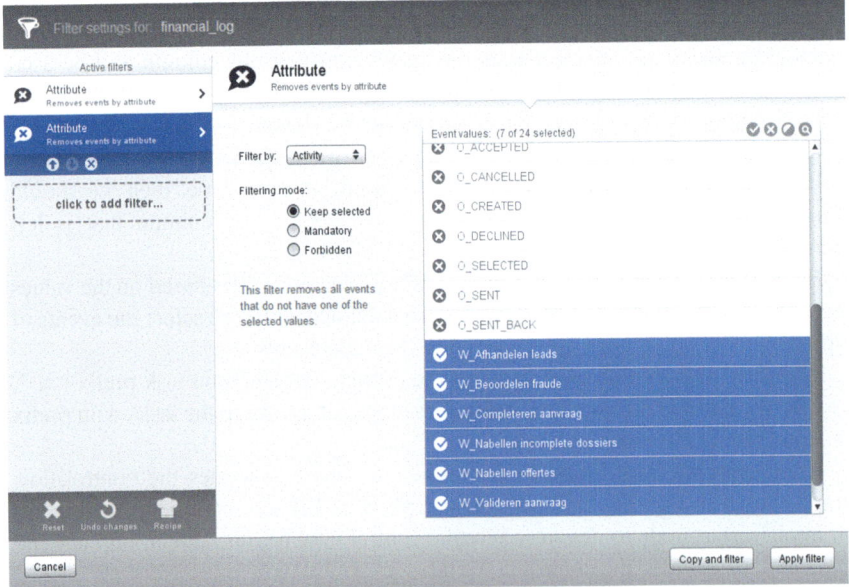

Fig. 28 Applying a filter on task name

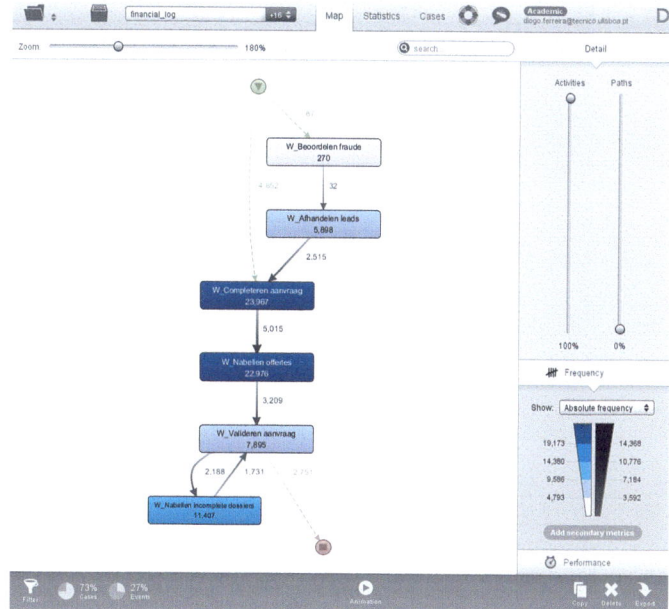

Fig. 29 Control-flow perspective in Disco

With the sliders shown on the right-hand side of Fig. 29, it is possible to do some post-processing on this graph, from showing only the most common nodes and edges to showing the control-flow graph in full detail.

In Fig. 29, the slider for *activities* (nodes) is at 100% and the slider for *paths* (edges) is at 0%. This means that, in principle, Disco should show every node but no edges. However, Disco does not leave nodes or process fragments dangling around without connections to other nodes. Therefore, despite having the *Paths* slider at 0%, Disco still shows the edges required to connect those nodes.

By moving the *Paths* slider to 100%, Disco will show the control-flow graph in full detail, with the same transition counts as in Fig. 22 on page 75.

Disco has also a performance perspective where it shows the time between events plotted over the same control-flow graph, as shown in Fig. 30. Disco is able to show the mean, median, minimum, maximum, and total time between events.

Note, however, that the results shown in Fig. 30 have been computed over the events coming from the application of the two filters in Figs. 27 and 28. This means that Disco is calculating the average timestamp difference between COMPLETE events. In particular, Disco is showing the mean time between the (last) COMPLETE event of one activity and the (first) COMPLETE event of the next activity. As we have seen before, in this event log each activity may comprise several COMPLETE events, so the results should be interpreted with care.

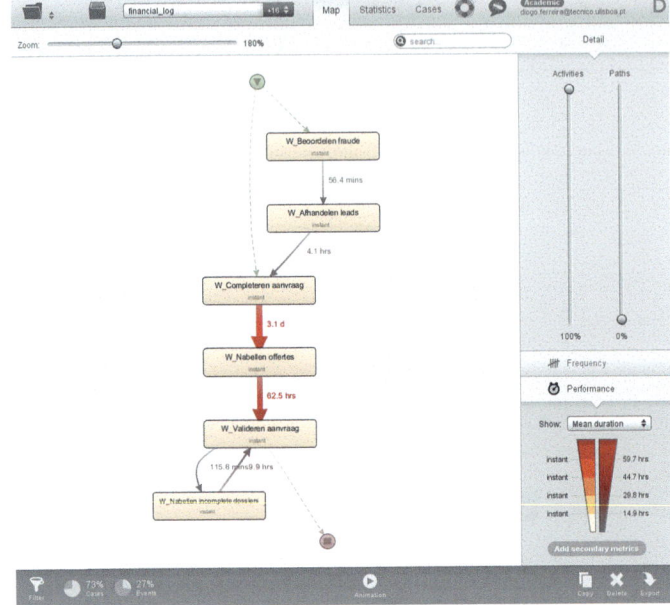

Fig. 30 Performance perspective in Disco

Disco includes several other functionalities, such as plotting the length of cases (both in terms of number of events and duration), and the number of occurrences of each task and user in the event log.

In addition, Disco includes an impressive log replay visualization, referred to as *animation*, where events are highlighted in the graph as they occurred over time (but in accelerated time, so that the whole event log can be replayed in a few minutes).

Finally, Disco can display the handover of work by an appropriate choice of columns (i.e. by choosing the user column as activity column). However, it does not support the working together perspective. For this and other advanced techniques, one can resort to a more sophisticated tool, namely ProM.

5.8   Process Mining with ProM

ProM[10] is the ultimate process mining toolbox. It was originally developed by the group of Prof. Wil van der Aalst at the Eindhoven University of Technology. Today, ProM includes several techniques developed by other research groups as well.

---

[10]http://www.promtools.org/.

In fact, ProM was devised with an extensible architecture in mind, allowing other people to contribute with the implementation of their own techniques, in the form of *plug-ins*. Hence, ProM is usually referred to as a *framework* [22].

At its core, the ProM framework is able to load event logs, run plug-ins, and display the results. When loading an event log, the preferred format is XES. Once an event log has been loaded, there are several different types of plug-ins that can be applied over it. For example:

- there are plug-ins to sort, convert, filter, and add information the event log;
- there are plug-ins to extract control-flow models, social networks, and other kinds of models from an event log;
- there are plug-ins to convert between different types of models and to analyze the properties of those models;
- there are plug-ins to check the conformance between a control-flow model and a given event log;
- etc.

The list of plug-ins available in ProM keeps growing, and ProM provides the framework to invoke any of these plug-ins on a given set of inputs, which typically consist in an event log, a model, or both.

A key feature of ProM is that the output of a plug-in (e.g. a filtered event log, or a control-flow model) can be used as input to other plug-ins. This way it becomes possible to carry out an analysis by applying a sequence of plug-ins.

For example, one could use a preprocessing plug-in to filter the input event log, then a mining plug-in to generate a control-flow model, and finally an analysis plug-in to analyze the structural properties of the generated model.

Traditionally, ProM is very geared towards the use of Petri nets as control-flow models. This is due both to historical and practical reasons. In the late 1990s, Wil van der Aalst wrote a seminal paper [17], which established Petri nets as the preferred language for modeling and analyzing workflows.

In fact, Petri nets provide a number of distinct advantages, the most important being that they have a mathematical foundation that enables formal analysis of structure and behavior. For example, it is possible to formally prove whether a Petri net has deadlocks or non-executable paths, among other properties.

This is the reason why many plug-ins in ProM work with Petri nets. There are mining plug-ins to generate Petri nets, and there are analysis plug-ins to check the properties of those Petri nets. There are also conversion plug-ins to convert Petri nets to and from other kinds of models.

Petri nets have also precise execution semantics (meaning that there is no doubt or ambiguity in how a given Petri net will execute). For this reason, Petri nets are the preferred model for conformance checking plug-ins based on log replay.

Figure 31 shows the workspace environment in ProM 6, after loading the event log from the BPI Challenge 2012. This workspace keeps the event logs, models, and other items that have been either imported or generated during the current session. Any of these items can be selected for further processing.

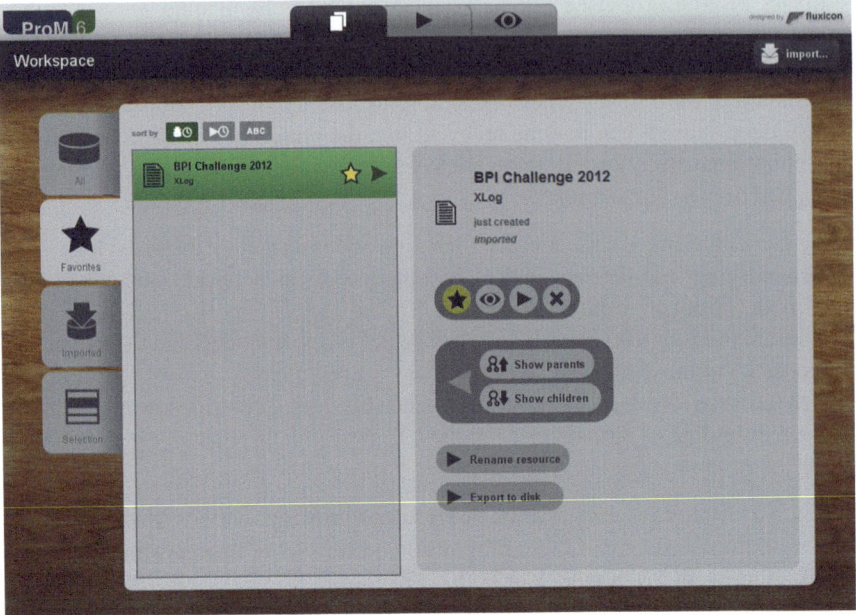

Fig. 31 The workspace environment in ProM

At the top of Fig. 31, there are three distinct tabs. Besides the *Workspace* tab, there is also the *Actions* tab and the *Views* tab. The *Actions* tab is where the user can select and run plug-ins. Figure 32 shows an example.

In Fig. 32, we have selected a filter to be applied to the event log. The selected plug-in (*Filter Log on Event Attribute Values*) allows filtering the events by task, user, timestamp, and event type.

As shown in Fig. 33, the filter configuration dialog has several tabs which correspond to the event attributes that are present in the XES log file (`concept:name`, `lifecycle:transition`, `org:resource`, and `time:timestamp`). In each of these tabs, it is possible to select the admissible values for each of those attributes.

For illustrative purposes, we will be selecting the events with prefix 'A_' in order to analyze the control flow of loan application states.

Back in Fig. 32, we can see that this filter plug-in will produce a new event log as output (as shown in the right-hand side of the figure). This new event log will be added to the workspace in Fig. 31, and from there it is possible to select it and use it as input to other plug-ins.

Here, the filtered event log will be used as input to a mining plug-in that will generate a Petri net. The specific plug-in that we will use (*Mine Petri net with Inductive Miner*) contains an implementation of a process discovery technique described in [6, 7]. In general, the details about each plug-in can be found in the literature. A link for more information is usually provided in the plug-in itself.

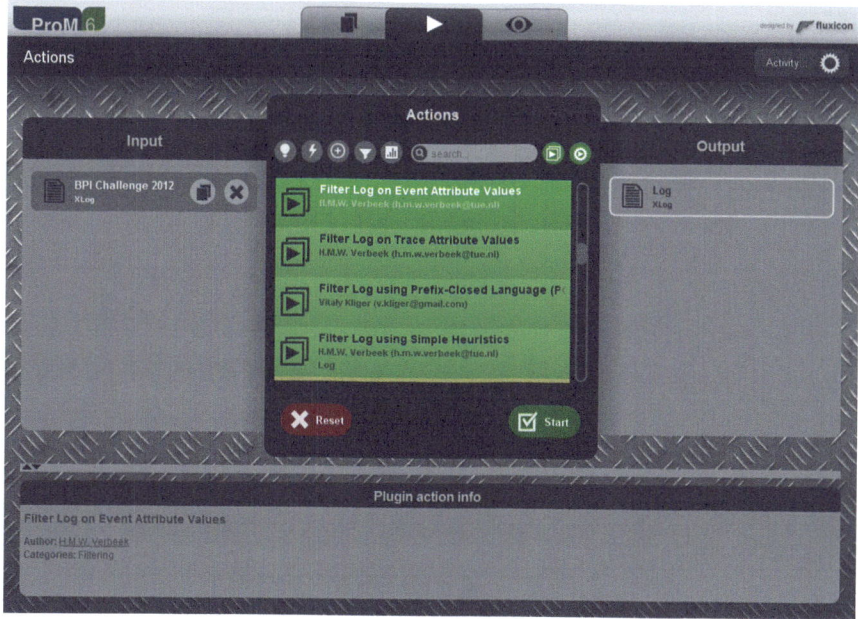

Fig. 32 Selecting a filter plug-in in ProM 6

Fig. 33 Configuring a filter plug-in in ProM 6

Fig. 34 Selecting a mining plug-in in ProM 6

As shown in Fig. 34, this plug-in receives an event log as input (left-hand side) and produces a Petri net as output (right-hand side), together with an initial marking and a final marking for the Petri net. These markings are relevant for some conformance checking plug-ins that are also available in ProM.

Figure 35 shows the Petri net that is generated by this mining plug-in, when using the default configuration parameters. It is interesting to note how this Petri net captures the behavior of A_REGISTERED, A_APPROVED, and A_ACTIVATED.

Earlier, from Fig. 20 on page 73, we had already concluded that these events can happen in any order, due to the mutual edges that exist between them. However, Fig. 35 shows this behavior in a much clearer way.

In Fig. 35, the circles represent *places* and the rectangles represent *transitions*. Places can have tokens, and in fact the first place in this Petri net is marked as having one token. When a transition fires, it removes one token from each of its input places, and it adds one token to each of its output places.

In general, each transition represents an activity in the process, and the firing of a transition corresponds to an event that has been recorded in the event log. In Fig. 35 there are also dark, filled rectangles which represent *silent transitions*.

Silent transitions do not correspond to actual activities, nor to events in the event log. They are introduced for the purpose of capturing the behavior of the process. For example, if one or more activities can be skipped, it is common to introduce a silent transition to be able to "jump over" those activities.

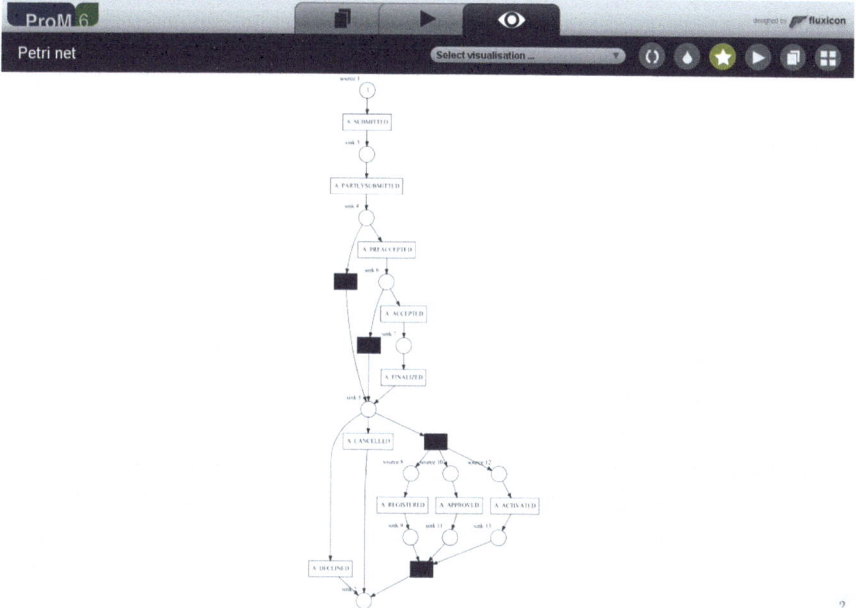

Fig. 35 Petri net generated by a mining plug-in in ProM 6

Silent transitions can also be used for the purpose of spawning and synchronizing multiple parallel paths, and this is precisely what is happening in the Petri net of Fig. 35 with A_REGISTERED, A_APPROVED, and A_ACTIVATED.

There is a silent transition that, when fired, adds tokens to the input places of those three activities. Afterwards, there is another silent transition that can only fire when there is a token in every output place of those activities.

In other words, those three activities run in parallel and can fire in any order. This is much more evident in Fig. 35 than in Fig. 20, and it serves to highlight one of the advantages of using Petri nets as control-flow models, which is their natural ability to capture parallel behavior.

Regarding the organizational perspective, Fig. 36 shows a visualization of the working together network, highlighting the fact that user 112 plays a central role, as we have already seen in Fig. 23 on page 76.

The social network in Fig. 36 is being displayed according to a ranking view, where the ranking is the degree (number of connections) of each node. Nodes in the periphery have a low degree, whereas nodes towards the center have an increasingly larger degree. Node 112 is positioned right at the center with the highest degree of all, since it connects to every other node.

Finally, Fig. 37 shows a dotted chart that can be used to carry out an analysis in the performance perspective. This chart was generated from the same filtered event log as before, so it contains only events with prefix 'A_'.

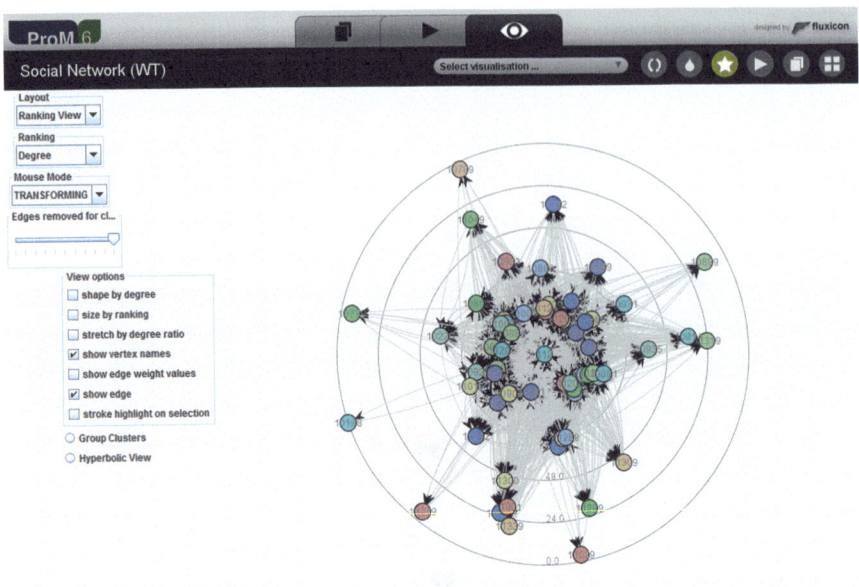

Fig. 36 Working together network generated by ProM 6

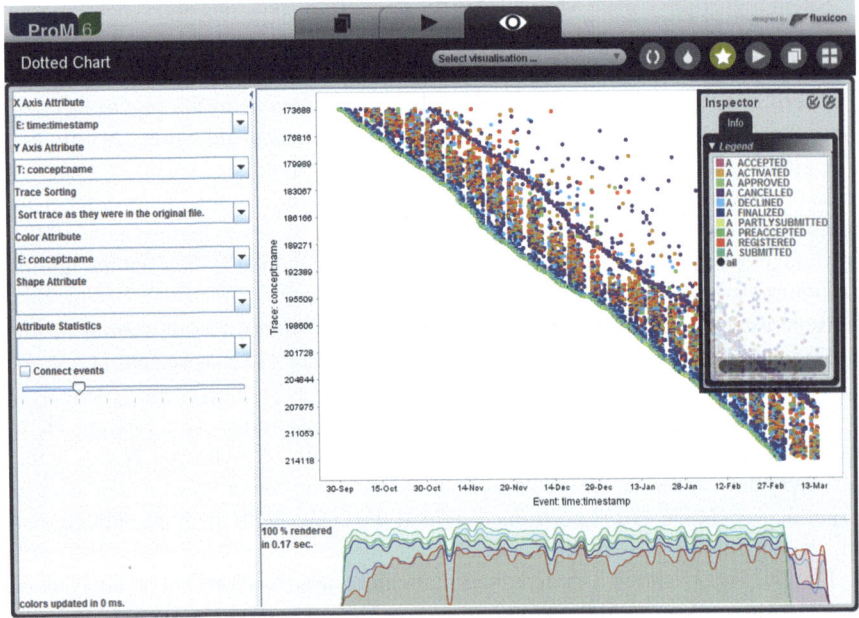

Fig. 37 Dotted chart generated by ProM 6

It is interesting to note that there seems to be a parallel trend in the behavior of A_CANCELLED with respect to the beginning of the process. This suggests that the cancellation of a loan application might be taking place automatically, after a certain period of time has elapsed (timeout).

It is also interesting to note that, from the vertical stripes in the chart, one can clearly distinguish between working days and weekends, including a period of slightly lower activity around Christmas and the New Year.

5.9 Conclusion

In this chapter, we picked up a real-world event log from a BPI Challenge, and we analyzed this event log with the techniques described in the previous chapters. We have also looked at two process mining tools: Disco and ProM. While doing this, we learned the following:

- There is a standard format for event logs (XES), which is an XML-based and extensible format that should be able to cater for present and future needs. ProM uses XES, and is able to filter an event log based on the attributes and extensions defined in that standard format.
- Real-world event logs have complex behaviors that are often difficult to understand. One way to deal with this complexity is to analyze separately certain subsets of events. These subsets can be obtained by applying filters over the event log. Both Disco and ProM support filters.
- ProM is the reference tool in the area of process mining. However, to take full advantage of ProM, one must be familiar with the underlying techniques behind a series of different plug-ins. Some of these plug-ins come from cutting-edge research. As an alternative, Disco is a more user-friendly tool.
- By analyzing a single perspective it can be difficult to explain the behavior observed in the event log. An integrated analysis of the three perspectives—control-flow, organizational, and performance—can provide better insights into the behavior of business processes.

Congratulations on having finished this book! If you got a good grasp of the techniques described herein, you can move on to more advanced literature, such as [18]. Also, have a look at http://processmining.org/, where you can find a lot of materials and can keep up with the latest developments in this field.

References

1. Dumas, M., La Rosa, M., Mendling, J., Reijers, H.: Fundamentals of Business Process Management. Springer, Berlin (2013)
2. Ferreira, D.R., Alves, C.: Discovering user communities in large event logs. In: BPM 2011 Workshops, Part I. LNBIP, vol. 99, pp. 123–134. Springer, Berlin (2012)
3. Ferreira, D.R., Vasilyev, E.: Using logical decision trees to discover the cause of process delays from event logs. Comput. Ind. **70**, 194–207 (2015)
4. Günther, C.W., van der Aalst, W.M.P.: Fuzzy mining – adaptive process simplification based on multi-perspective metrics. In: Business Process Management. Lecture Notes in Computer Science, vol. 4714, pp. 328–343. Springer, Berlin (2007)
5. Han, J., Kamber, M., Pei, J.: Data Mining: Concepts and Techniques, 3rd edn. Morgan Kaufmann, San Francisco (2012)
6. Leemans, S.J.J., Fahland, D., van der Aalst, W.M.P.: Discovering block-structured process models from event logs – a constructive approach. In: Application and Theory of Petri Nets and Concurrency. Lecture Notes in Computer Science, vol. 7927, pp. 311–329. Springer, Berlin (2013)
7. Leemans, S.J.J., Fahland, D., van der Aalst, W.M.P.: Discovering block-structured process models from event logs containing infrequent behaviour. In: Business Process Management Workshops. LNBIP, vol. 171, pp. 66–78. Springer, Cham (2014)
8. Mans, R.S., Schonenberg, M.H., Song, M., van der Aalst, W.M.P., Bakker, P.J.M.: Application of process mining in healthcare – a case study in a dutch hospital. In: Biomedical Engineering Systems and Technologies. CCIS, vol. 25, pp. 425–438. Springer, Berlin (2009)
9. de Medeiros, A.K.A., Weijters, A.J.M.M., van der Aalst, W.M.P.: Genetic process mining: an experimental evaluation. Data Min. Knowl. Disc. **14**(2), 245–304 (2007)
10. Nakatumba, J., van der Aalst, W.M.P.: Analyzing resource behavior using process mining. In: Business Process Management Workshops. LNBIP, vol. 43, pp. 69–80 (2010)
11. Newman, M.E.J.: Modularity and community structure in networks. PNAS **103**(23), 8577–8582 (2006)
12. Rozinat, A., van der Aalst, W.: Conformance checking of processes based on monitoring real behavior. Inf. Syst. **33**(1), 64–95 (2008)
13. Scott, J.: Social Network Analysis. SAGE, Thousand Oaks (2013)
14. Song, M., van der Aalst, W.: Supporting process mining by showing events at a glance. In: Proceedings of 17th Annual Workshop on Information Technologies and Systems (WITS 2007). pp. 139–145. Montreal, Canada (December 2007)
15. Song, M., van der Aalst, W.M.: Towards comprehensive support for organizational mining. Decis. Support. Syst. **46**(1), 300–317 (2008)

© The Author(s) 2020
D. R. Ferreira, *A Primer on Process Mining*, SpringerBriefs in Information Systems, https://doi.org/10.1007/978-3-030-41819-9

16. Vaisman, A., Zimányi, E.: Data Warehouse Systems: Design and Implementation. Springer, Berlin (2014)
17. van der Aalst, W.M.P.: The application of petri nets to workflow management. J. Circ. Syst. Comput. **8**(1), 21–66 (1998)
18. van der Aalst, W.: Process Mining: Data Science in Action, 2nd edn. Springer, Berlin (2016)
19. van der Aalst, W.M.P., Weijters, A.J.M.M., Maruster, L.: Workflow mining: discovering process models from event logs. IEEE Trans. Knowl. Data Eng. **16**, 1128–1142 (2004)
20. van der Aalst, W.M.P., Reijers, H.A., Song, M.: Discovering social networks from event logs. Comput. Supported Coop. Work **14**(6), 549–593 (2005)
21. van Dongen, B.F., van der Aalst, W.M.P.: A meta model for process mining data. In: EMOI-INTEROP'05: Enterprise Modelling and Ontologies for Interoperability. CEUR Workshop Proceedings, vol. 160 (2005)
22. van Dongen, B.F., de Medeiros, A.A., Verbeek, H., Weijters, A., van der Aalst, W.: The ProM framework: a new era in process mining tool support. In: Applications and Theory of Petri Nets 2005. Lecture Notes in Computer Science, vol. 3536, pp. 444–454. Springer, Berlin (2005)
23. Verbeek, H.M.W., Buijs, J.C.A.M., van Dongen, B.F., van der Aalst, W.M.P.: XES, XESame, and ProM 6. In: Information Systems Evolution. LNBIP, vol. 72, pp. 60–75. Springer, Heidelberg (2011)
24. Wasserman, S., Faust, K.: Social Network Analysis: Methods and Applications. Cambridge University Press, Cambridge (1994)
25. Weijters, A.J.M.M., van der Aalst, W.M.P., de Medeiros, A.K.A.: Process mining with the HeuristicsMiner algorithm. Tech. Rep. WP 166, Eindhoven University of Technology (2006)
26. Wen, L., Wang, J., van der Aalst, W.M.P., Huang, B., Sun, J.: A novel approach for process mining based on event types. J. Intell. Inf. Syst. **32**(2), 163–190 (2009)
27. Weske, M.: Business Process Management: Concepts, Languages, Architectures, 2nd edn. Springer, Berlin (2012)

The manufacturer's authorised representative in the EU is Springer
Nature Customer Service Centre GmbH, Europaplatz 3, 69115 Heidelberg,
Germany. If you have any concerns regarding our products, please
contact ProductSafety@springernature.com

Printed and bound by CPI Group (UK) Ltd, Croydon, CR0 4YY

29/04/2026

02099459-0011